SCOTLAND'S HISTORY

Fiona Watson

SCOTLAND'S HISTORY

Published in 2020 by Historic Environment Scotland
Enterprises Limited SC510997

HISTORIC ENVIRONMENT SCOTLAND | ARAINNEACHD EACHDRAIDHEIL ALBA

Historic Environment Scotland
Longmore House
Salisbury Place
Edinburgh
EH9 1SH

Registered Charity SC045925
British Library Cataloguing-in-Publication Data. A catalogue
record for this book is available from the British Library.
ISBN 978 1 84917 307 0
© Fiona Watson 2020

Typeset in Gotham and Gill Sans
Printed and bound in Italy by Elcograf S.p.A.

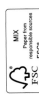

MIX
Paper from
responsible sources
FSC
FSC®
www.fsc.org

contents

INTRODUCTION

Scotland's vibrant and bloody past captures the imagination, inspiring books and films, its many picturesque ruins making wonderful photographs. But there is far more to Scottish history than murder and mayhem, tragedy and betrayal. In the following pages, we will fly through thousands of years of impressive achievement and painful change, a journey that will take us all over the country and into the homes and lives of kings and queens, nobles and churchmen, peasants and townsfolk. The panoramas beneath our gaze will alter before our eyes thanks to a potent blend of natural and human forces forever at work even when old habits and beliefs seemed reassuringly eternal. There was nothing inevitable about much of it, but these deep layers of past experience, landscapes and physical remains have created something unique and precious that underlies what we mean by Scotland and the Scots.

Scotia map, c1560 The first printed map of Scotland, engraved by the Italian cartographer Paolo Forlani. Reproduced by permission of the National Library of Scotland. Based on an earlier map by George Lily.

CHAPTER ONE

SETTLING IN 9500 BC–AD 89

Compared with the history of our planet, Scotland is a newcomer. Even within the history of our own species, we must start quite recently – around 10,000 years ago – for we have nothing left to tell us what came before thanks to the deeply destructive forces unleashed by the last Ice Age (c31,000 BC–c9500 BC).

Even once the climate began to warm and the ice to melt, it still took a thousand years or so for the first intrepid humans to venture this far north, crossing the land bridge that connected Britain to Europe. Already the warming climate had transformed the land from rubble-strewn plains of tough, shrubby plants filled with great beasts like the woolly mammoth into a well-wooded landscape housing a wealth of smaller animals and birds, including bear, wolf and lynx.

The early settlers were hunter gatherers. The fit and healthy moved around large swathes of territory, depending on the season, to collect the fruits of the forest and the rivers and seas. What little imprint they made on the landscape has mostly disappeared, though they certainly cut down trees and surely understood how to use fire and other techniques to get what they needed – food, fodder, shelter and

Ring of Brodgar, Orkney The c4,000-year-old Ring of Brodgar, one of many incredible ceremonial monuments on Orkney, sits on a narrow strip of land surrounded by sea and sky. HES

implements – from the forest. With the exception of a few structures, all they have left behind for us to find are their tools – broad-bladed pieces of flint – and huge and numerous 'middens' – rubbish heaps made up mostly of the discarded remains of shellfish.

But some 6,000 years ago a radically new way of living and working, of taming and using the environment, finally made its way to this north-western corner of Europe, this time from the Near East. The adoption of farming – domesticating strains of wild cereals and animals for human food production – is one of the most profound and enduring transformations we have ever wrought on our species and the world around us. New arrivals, descended from peoples who originally came from modern Turkey, headed west via the Mediterranean bringing these new ideas with them.

And yet the advantages were not necessarily obvious to our hunter-gatherer forebears, since growing crops and raising animals in one place was a high risk, labour-intensive strategy, which, if it failed, brought utter ruin. Many probably continued with the old ways, co-existing with those prepared to risk the new practices. But once early farmers started to settle in one place,

Old Scatness, Shetland
This reconstructed roundhouse shows the kind of home built throughout Scotland (with regional differences) from around 700 BC to AD 500.
Davy Cooper, Shetland Amenity Trust.

Skara Brae, Orkney
Older than the pyramids and perhaps inhabited for 600 years, this Neolithic settlement was uncovered once again following a storm in 1850. HES

they began to leave more and more traces of their presence, as the superb stone village at Skara Brae in Orkney proudly illustrates, though the remains of their timber halls and huts are no more than shadows on the ground.

The grandest remains from this period reflect the belief systems that bound these communities together, no doubt displaying complex ideas about the relationship between the here and now and what lay beyond. These could be huge structures stretching over several kilometres, as at Cleaven Dyke in Perthshire, or more compact but equally awe-inspiring monuments such as Maeshowe and the Ring of Brodgar in Orkney or the Calanais standing stones in Lewis. They are testament to the power these early farmers wielded over the landscape and their desire to flaunt it for miles around, as well as their ability to work together – whether voluntarily or when ordered to.

But around 4,500 years ago, a new wave of incomers arrived whose ancestors had headed west from the Great Steppes that link Europe with Asia. These Beaker people brought new technologies, including domesticated horses

Calanais standing stones, Lewis
Around 5,000 years old, this extraordinary monument comprises a long avenue leading to a stone circle with a burial cairn in the middle. HES

and wheeled vehicles, as well as their own distinctive pottery (the 'beakers' for which they are now known). Armed with such powerful innovations, they spread across these islands, almost completely displacing those already there.

So it is not very surprising that these social changes led to the end of the communal burial places which had afforded each community the protection of their ancestors, replaced by smaller tombs housing the remains of one individual, presumably a war leader or chief. The Beaker people clearly did not like vast communal projects and had little interest in the ancestors of the native tribes. Instead they seem to have preferred to harness teams of labourers to build small stone circles, which sprang up in large numbers, particularly in the north-east, after 2500 BC.

Despite all these changes, Scotland's population was still tiny and spread across the country, even remarkably high up into the hills. During the first millennium BC, the climate turned wetter and colder, the waterlogged ground transformed into the peat that still covers much of the Scottish uplands. Such soils have their uses, not least for giving a distinctive taste to Scottish whisky, but are no good for living and working on.

Upland settlements were abandoned, while the valleys became unhelpfully boggy. Those farming the land in between were in the best place, building sturdy wooden fences or stone walls in and around their settlements to protect themselves from outside threats and their crops from being trampled by their animals.

At the same time, ostentatious chiefly residences across the country began to follow regional patterns. Brochs – double-walled stone towers with a hollow middle as at Gurness in Orkney, Glenelg opposite Skye and Mousa in Shetland – emerged in the far north and north-west, while distinctive types of hill-fort were built in the mid-west, as at Dunadd, and the south-east, such as at Habchester in the Borders. Across western and central Scotland crannogs also appeared – circular structures built on artificial islands or stilts in lakes and rivers, a style of settlement that remained useful for many thousands of years.

The people who lived in these impressive, complex dwellings demanded the respect and the labour of those beneath them. Their

Mousa Broch, Shetland
Standing 13 metres high, this magnificent hollow tower or broch is a type of Iron Age architecture found only in Scotland. HES SC1670313

Habchester Fort, Borders

This Iron Age fort, divided between two landowners, shows clearly the impact of ploughing on ancient monuments. HES SC993205

Crannog on Loch Tay, Perthshire
This reconstruction shows an elite Iron Age dwelling at a time when travel by water was much easier than by land.
Scottish Viewpoint / Alamy.

job was to protect those who accepted their authority, as well as the resources that sustained them all. As we move into the first millennium after the birth of Christ in faraway Roman Judea, there is evidence that such chiefs already held sway over territories that ranged further than their immediate kin-group and that they might use extreme violence against those who challenged them or who had what they wanted.

CHAPTER TWO
TRIBES, ROMANS, SAINTS AND KINGS 79–900

Once they wielded power beyond their own tribes, some native warlords felt confident enough to live in settlements without walls. But they were about to face a much more imposing enemy. Over 1,500 miles from Scotland, the seeds of one of the world's greatest empires had been sown with the founding of the city of Rome around 753 BC. The first Roman armies reached southern Britain almost exactly seven hundred years later, but it was not until AD 79 that a fleet was sent to map the northern parts of the island as preparation for conquest.

Campaigns were launched in AD 83, 141 and 200, with legions building forts, camps, roads and the accoutrements of Roman military life right across southern Scotland and as far north-east as Kirriemuir in Angus. But with the need to pour money into other parts of the Empire often reducing the resources available at its northernmost limit, it proved impossible to bring most of Scotland under permanent imperial control. Instead the Romans built barriers between themselves and the native tribes who resisted them – Hadrian's Wall in northern England in AD 122 and the Antonine Wall between the

St Columba, Iona Abbey This statue is on the site of Columba's original monastery, founded in AD 563. It became one of Britain and Ireland's most important religious sites. HES

rivers Forth and Clyde in central Scotland twenty years later.

But the Romans certainly had an effect on Scotland. Many of the tribes just beyond the walls happily joined trading networks stretching across the world as they knew it. A huge horde of hacksilver (silverware chopped into precise units of weight at a time of crisis when hard cash was scarce) buried on Traprain Law east of Edinburgh shows us the wealth that doing business with the Empire could bring, even as it began to contract and implode. And then there were the Roman roads, many of which were still in use more than a thousand years later.

But the most profound and enduring changes only took hold once the legions finally left Britain in AD 411. The first was the gradual adoption of Christianity as the dominant religion by those living in the British Isles and Ireland from the sixth century. Previously it had been confined to pockets of believers who had converted once it became the official religion of Rome in the fourth century. In AD 563 the Irish saint Columba founded his famous monastery on the island of Iona thanks to a gift from the king of Dál Riata, a kingdom encompassing modern Argyll and the southern Hebrides which

The Antonine Wall, Stirlingshire

A second Roman invasion of Scotland took place on Antoninus's orders in AD 141, resulting in the building of the Antonine Wall between the Forth and Clyde estuaries. HES

**Iona Abbey,
Inner Hebrides**
As a major centre of
learning, Iona was renowned
throughout Britain and
beyond and is still a focus of
pilgrimage today. HES

had close links with Ireland and spoke the same Gaelic language. However, Columba went on only one mission – to try to convert the Pictish king of Fortriu (the area around Inverness). Though he failed, Christianity soon took root north of the Grampian Mountains. St Ninian – which is almost certainly a corruption of the Irish name Finnian, which equates to the name Uinniau used by the Britons – had more success earlier in the sixth century with the leaders of the kingdoms of southern Pictland. The worship of a single God, along with religious practices promoting hierarchy and the centralisation of power, appealed to warlords interested in the same things.

The spread of Christianity complements an important legacy of the Roman presence in Britain, namely that resisting Rome brought some tribes together into larger groupings. Though, as we've seen, the natives of the British Isles were largely descendants of the Beaker people, the Romans labelled those separated by their walls with different identities. The Britons lived in Roman Britain, while those 'from across the sea' (presumably the River Forth) were Picts and the inhabitants of Dál Riata in the far west were Scots, a name they shared with the Irish.

But we shouldn't imagine them as single tribal groupings as yet.

Beyond the River Forth after the Roman withdrawal, fortified enclosures and settlements – especially hill-forts – came back into use, often reoccupying earlier sites. This probably relates to the emergence of the first kings in mainland Scotland from the sixth century, an even greater assumption of power for fewer individuals manifesting itself in a desire once again to show off their status in impressive lofty citadels.

At the same time, there was a revived interest in building monuments to the dead. They incorporated Christian elements into existing ritual landscapes, emphasising a direct relationship with ancient pagan ancestors who gave current chiefs and kings access to the supernatural. Though many centuries later the Roman Catholic Church would insist that only priests had such powers, many of the ceremonies presided over by the newly Christian rulers of these early kingdoms were not necessarily very different to pre-Christian rituals. In a time of much change, the past was essential to explaining the present.

But it was not all plain sailing. Many of the revamped forts from this period only get a

The Drosten Stone
The back of this carved Pictish cross-slab shows various intriguing symbols, as well as animals such as eagle, doe, salmon, bear and wild boar.
HES SC579211

mention in the historical record because they were attacked or captured, whether in the western Scottish kingdom of Dál Riata, the Pictish kingdoms of much of the mainland, the kingdom of Britons in the south-west centred on Dumbarton on the River Clyde or the kingdoms of the advancing Anglo-Saxons south of the River Forth. The Anglo-Saxons, who had first invaded England in the fifth century, tried to get further north, but were stopped in their tracks when they were defeated by the northern Pictish king of Fortriu at the Battle of Nechtansmere in May 685.

But in more peaceful times, the residents of these power centres enjoyed trading links with Europe as well as the rest of Britain and Ireland. They presided over the manipulation of the local landscape for farming and important ceremonial events, and provided a home and patronage for specialised craftspeople producing the high-end bling – brooches, belt buckles, ornaments for horses – beloved of the warrior class and their families. And not all forts were built on easily defended hill-top sites, as the low-lying and spectacularly enclosed 'palace' at Rhynie in north-east Scotland and later royal residence at Forteviot near Perth make clear.

Making sense of the Picts – There is much to perplex us about the Picts. Originally the inhabitants beyond the Antonine Wall were lumped under the term Caledonians by the Romans, as well as their particular tribal names. But by the end of the Roman period, the northern natives were described as Picts – 'painted people'. Alas, the Picts have left no written record, though they were certainly literate. Instead their beautiful carved stones serve to tell us much about their beliefs and way of life.

A number of Pictish kingdoms lay between the River Forth and the far northern coast. But, from the seventh century, the rulers of one of them – Fortriu, based around Inverness – became super-kings. The catalyst was their victory at the battle of Nechtansmere (AD 685), which not only halted Anglo-Saxon expansion but allowed them to extend their authority over the other Pictish kingdoms south of the Grampian Mountains. Then, from the 720s, they proved powerful enough to be able to install their own choices as client kings of the Gaelic kingdom of Dál Riata at the other end of the Great Glen from Inverness.

The kings of Fortriu also benefited from a change in the European barter trade in prestige goods, which had moved away from the Atlantic seaways favouring Dál Riata to more exclusive use of the North Sea to which they had easy access. This probably explains why the tiny monastery at Portmahomack north of Inverness was transformed into a major ecclesiastical centre in the eighth century, where craftspeople made stunning glass and metal objects for celebrating the Mass and vellum for the writing of scripture – exactly the kind of goods that could be traded across Europe.

But by the beginning of the ninth century, both Fortriu and Dál Riata proved vulnerable to the Norse crossing the North Sea in search of plunder and then new homes. This set the scene for the formation of the kingdom of Scotland, ruled by Gaels from Dál Riata, but situated in the former Pictish kingdoms.

A painted 'Pict' Many artists have been inspired by the fact that 'Pict' is derived from the Latin word for painted — this engraving was based on artwork by John White, a colonist who also painted watercolours of the New World. Bridgeman Images. From *Grands Voyages*, report of a journey to Virginia in 1585. Engraved by Theodore de Bry.

the picts

As for everybody else, the routine of the farming year and the dictates of the weather would, as ever, be uppermost in people's minds. Where stone was plentiful and timber scarce (in the Northern Isles and the Hebrides), small cellular houses of various designs evolved into a roughly standard figure-of-eight form. Timber was the building material of choice elsewhere, leaving little trace, but there is evidence for the building of longhouses in central Scotland. These were perhaps on an Anglo-Saxon model, with turf walls and a pit or drain in the end that housed the animals.

Farming remained much the same as it had for thousands of years. Technology had not advanced beyond the basic ard plough, its cutting blade making a shallow groove without turning over the soil. Over time, such ploughing could create lynchets (great ridges formed on the downhill side of a field) or cord rig (regular furrows with the channels used for drainage).

Barley was the main crop planted across Scotland, along with oats, though some farmers were able to grow wheat and its variant, spelt. Rotary querns, which ground corn between a static lower stone and a top stone that could be turned, were commonly used. The cultivated

Huntsman from a Pictish grave-marker
Hunting images such as this mounted hunter are characteristic of Pictish sculpture. HES. Linocut of carving found at Kirriemuir, Angus.

ground might be moved about from time to time in order to give the land a rest, with temporary field boundaries or ditches used to keep animals out of the fields.

But while this kind of farming kept most people occupied and fed, it was cattle – and the raids that kept the warrior class busy in acquiring more of the livestock (not to mention slaves) – that testified to the wealth of a man and a people in this patriarchal society, not least as protection against famine. Cows were possibly also used as compensation for crimes resulting in death or injury, as certainly became the case in the tenth and eleventh centuries.

The nobility of northern Britain were expert horsemen and women, who loved to hunt the wild beasts found on the moors and in the forests, often, in the case of the Picts, celebrating their prowess on beautiful carved standing stones. Though the lynx had recently died out, brown bear were still to be found in Scotland (though for only a few more centuries), along with deer, wild boar, wild ox, wolves and birds like the majestic golden eagle and the capercaillie. Hunting kept the warrior agile, his eye keen. And none more so than the northern Pictish kings of Fortriu.

The rise of these kings to pre-eminence is reflected in changes to elite power centres throughout the territories under their overall control, including Dál Riata. Many smaller forts were abandoned in favour of a select few larger, more complex fortified sites. These strongholds might be focused on an inner sanctum at the very top, with terraces and enclosures of lesser importance spiralling down below, as at Dunadd in Dál Riata and Dundurn in Perthshire. There could be no mistaking the importance of the man who presided over the highest compound, his prestige and authority visible for miles around, but access to his person was restricted to the chosen few. Within Fortriu itself, smaller hill-forts like the one at Craig Phadrig outside Inverness were abandoned in favour of more impressive residences, including the spectacular coastal fortress at Burghead near Elgin.

But even the kings of Fortriu proved no match for a new threat to all the peoples living on this north-western tip of Europe, which sailed into view from the north-east from the 790s. To begin with the Norse in their longships were intent on plunder, heading for the great monasteries – at Portmahomack, Iona and Lindisfarne off Anglo-Saxon Northumberland – and their treasures.

**Dunadd Fort,
Argyll and Bute**
This impressive hill-fort was probably the main stronghold and inauguration site of the kings of Dál Riata, the Gaelic-speaking kingdom in western Scotland. HES

But within a few generations these newcomers decided to settle down, mostly along the coast and on the islands of the north and west of Scotland, although they penetrated the south too. This made it far easier to raid across Britain and Ireland and they posed a significant threat to both Fortriu and Dál Riata. In 839, the king of Fortriu, the client king of Dál Riata and numerous others were killed in a great battle against the Norse.

The power of Fortriu was smashed, while Dál Riata disintegrated into civil war. After a few years of turmoil, a Gael of unknown origins named Kenneth MacAlpin (Cináed mac Alpín) took over Dál Riata's kingship. And a few years after that, he moved east out of the Norse danger zone to become king of the Picts too, based not in Fortriu, which was too vulnerable to attack, but in the safer lands south of the Grampian Mountains.

What happened next was certainly not inevitable, but the seeds of a new kingdom had been sown over the preceding 150 years thanks to the Pictish over-kingship assumed and promoted by the kings of Fortriu, as well as the challenge to the status quo posed by the Norse. But, contrary to popular belief, Kenneth

MacAlpin was not the first king of Scotland since it took time after his move into southern Pictland for the new kingdom to evolve out of the cataclysmic events of the ninth century. The first king to be designated 'of Scotland' was Kenneth's grandson, Donald, who died in 900. Perhaps these Gaelic-speaking refugees from Norse attacks on Dál Riata wished to avoid friction with their new subjects by giving their kingdom a new name, using the Gaelic word for Britain – Alba. It lay beyond the River Forth and as far north and west as the Norse would permit. Whether it would survive, in whole or in part, was another matter altogether.

Viking Ships, Sognefjord
This nineteenth-century imagining of a Norse longship highlights the seamanship of those great warrior sailors over 1,000 years earlier.
Copyright O Vaering / Bridgeman Images.
Watercolour by Hans Gude.

CHAPTER THREE
MAKING SCOTLAND 900–1286

We should not imagine this new Scotland as a unified, centralised kingdom like a modern nation state. For a start, the southern Pictish kingdoms, even when the northern king of Fortriu became their overlord, had never been one political unit with a common identity. Laws reflected various older customs and justice was administered locally. And though the king no doubt received contributions from his subjects towards his upkeep – in hospitality or goods, not money, for Scotland did not yet have its own coinage – it is not clear what his responsibilities were.

But we do know that ceremonies marking the creation of a king were already many centuries old. From c850 they were associated with the moot hill at Scone, north of Perth, and the Stone of Destiny on which the kings were inaugurated. Scotland's ruler and his senior nobility probably met but rarely, for there were surely few national issues on which he needed their advice or consent. Rather, his chief advisors usually came from a close-knit circle of relatives and friends, as well as Scotland's senior churchmen.

It might be supposed that the king could call out men to fight for him, though later sources suggest that any large-scale

Melrose Abbey, Borders Founded in 1136 by the Cistercians, one of the new, reformed monastic orders of the later Middle Ages, the abbey was extremely wealthy. HES

mobilisation had to be in self-defence. However, he and his nobility certainly joined forces to go on raids, though whether this was just the king and his friends or a wider group of nobles is anyone's guess. These warriors had raided to the south from at least the mid-ninth century, away from the Norse into the Anglo-Saxon kingdoms of Northumbria beyond the River Forth. On a good day, they brought back the usual cattle and slaves and were praised for their bravery and prowess.

But the Scots also had conquest in mind, decisively acquiring the northern part of the Northumbrian kingdom from the River Forth to the River Tweed by 1018. They also had their eye on their neighbour to the south-west, Strathclyde, a kingdom of Britons that once stretched from the River Clyde to Morecombe Bay over 150 miles further south (the native Britons having been pushed west over previous centuries by the invading Anglo-Saxons). By the early eleventh century, the top portion of Strathclyde down to the Solway Firth had also been acquired by Scotland's kings, giving them greater access to the important shipping lanes of the Irish Sea.

Beyond the Grampian Mountains that stretch from the north-east down to the west coast, Fortriu staggered on, still threatened by the

The Stone of Destiny
Taken by Edward I in 1296 and now on display in Edinburgh Castle, the Stone of Destiny was reputedly the biblical Jacob's Pillow. HES

Norse in Ireland and other parts of mainland Britain. Its leaders were probably members of Kenneth MacAlpin's family and initially formed part of the new Scottish kingdom under the Gaelic name of Moray. But leadership seems to have moved to another family and, while reluctantly acknowledging the Scottish kings as their rulers, they did not have an easy relationship with their southern overlords. By AD 1000 Moray was no longer viewed as part of the kingdom of Scotland.

But what of the vast majority who now, whether they liked it or not, belonged to a new kingdom where Gaelic was spoken? The Pictish language (or languages) died out, along with their particular styles of ornamentation for standing stones, but otherwise we know little about this profound upheaval. It is likely that some noble families were ousted by incoming Gaels, but the peasantry surely stayed where they were, doing what they'd always done.

The first king of Alba (Scotland) was Donald (889–900), Kenneth MacAlpin's grandson. Exactly why the word 'Alba' – which is the Gaelic word for Britain – was adopted is unclear, but it may mark the end of the process of turning Pictland into a Gaelic kingdom. Like their Irish relatives, the Gaelic-speaking rulers of Scotland practised a form of inheritance called tanistry. This meant rotating the kingship between two branches of the royal family, descendants of Kenneth MacAlpin's sons Constantine (862–77) and Aed (877–8). Such a rotation almost guaranteed that an adult male would take the crown, a necessity in such violent times.

But as the generations passed and the two branches became only distantly related, the temptation for the tanist (heir) to hasten the day of his crowning by attacking the current king became irresistible. Even when Aed's line died out in 997, it all began again within the line of Constantine, the relatives and retainers of each branch no doubt egging their man on. Reign lengths got shorter and more violent, which perhaps explains why there is little or no discernible artistic activity – which kings and nobles paid for – in this period.

Malcolm II (1005–34) decided to try to put an end to this volatility, though he could only do so because he won a dramatic victory against the Northumbrians at Carham in 1018. With his reputation riding high, he insisted his grandson Duncan should inherit the throne rather than the young cousin who was the designated heir from the other branch of the family. Realising he would be killed, this tanist (whose identity is a matter of some debate) made an alliance with the rulers of Moray, who also claimed the Scottish throne. This alliance was sealed by the marriage of the tanist's sister, Gruoch, to Gillacomgain of Moray.

It didn't work, not least because Moray was also in the grip of a bloodfeud within its own ruling family. The tanist was murdered and Duncan duly inherited the throne from his grandfather in 1034, keeping the succession within one dynasty. However, only six years later he faced another challenge from Moray. Sailing north, Duncan met his adversary at Pitgaveny near Elgin and was defeated. Now it was the victor's turn to be made king. Cousin to Gillacomgain, and married to his widow Gruoch, his name was Macbeth.

There can be no doubt that spreading rights to the throne across branches of the royal family was causing profound instability. But it was not easy to bring it within one dynasty. Macbeth managed it briefly, the kingship passing to his step-son Lulach (1058), but it was the man who killed them both – Malcolm III (1058–93) – who finally succeeded. Having said that, it was only with David I (1124–53), the youngest of Malcolm's five sons, that tentative steps were taken towards adopting primogeniture (inheritance by the oldest son). Even so, it did not finally happen until 1214, and even then there were challenges from other branches of the family until the middle of the thirteenth century.

Primogeniture was not the only innovation that David I introduced to Scotland. Brought up in England, he saw at first-hand the many features of (comparatively) intensive Norman government (England having been conquered by the Duke of Normandy in 1066), as well as new forms of ecclesiastical organisation, and was keen to encourage some of these systems to develop in Scotland.

While infighting at the very top was no doubt of little interest to most Scots, some of these twelfth-century innovations had a profound effect. The most important seems the most mundane, for the Normans brought to Britain the mould-board plough, which cut long, thick grooves and turned the soil right over, killing weeds and moving moisture away from the surface of the fields.

This revolution also brought about a move away from enclosed fields to an open 'runrig' system, named after the new broad strips of

Macbeth

The real Macbeth was a remarkable monarch – the only Scottish king to go on pilgrimage to Rome and a moderniser who was well-loved by his contemporaries.
HES. Portrait of Macbeth by Jacob de Wet II, c1684.

Murder Most Foul? Macbeth, King and Myth – The real Scottish king was the opposite of his fictional namesake. For a start, his 17-year reign (1040–57) was much longer than many of his predecessors. Macbeth can also claim a number of firsts: he kept Scotland largely peaceful; he was the only Scottish king to go on pilgrimage to Rome; and he persuaded a number of Norman knights to come north to act as his household guard, making him less beholden to friends and family. Even the man who killed him and took his throne – Duncan's son, Malcolm III – agreed he was a generous, well-loved king. But none of that mattered once the wars with England broke out in the thirteenth and fourteenth centuries, for then it became politically vital to portray a direct line of Scottish kings stretching back far beyond Kenneth MacAlpin. Macbeth's ancestors belonged to a different dynasty and so he was portrayed as a usurper. Not only that, but he hailed from Moray, a region which came to be viewed as a hotbed of rebellion. Almost all the stories about him that appear in Shakespeare's 'Scottish play' were written by the Scots themselves, although not composed quite so sublimely.

macbeth

Kelso Abbey, Borders
One of Scotland's largest and richest abbeys, Kelso was founded in 1128 close to the major royal castle at Roxburgh. HES. Engraving from *Border Antiquities of England and Scotland* Volume II by Sir Walter Scott.

ridges and furrows. Farmers could own a certain number of strips within the huge, open fields, but not any particular ones; instead they balloted each year so that everyone took their share of the best and the worst land. Teams of oxen could also be held communally to keep costs down.

On the downside, lords following Norman practices demanded far more duties and payments from their peasants, from forcing them to grind corn in their mills (and pay for the privilege) to demanding their free labour at various times of the year. And while the new plough must have improved yields, the runrig system stifled individual investment and further innovation, for the strips of land would pass to someone else the following year.

Other forms of agricultural innovation came from the new ecclesiastical orders introduced by David I, for they viewed it as their duty to make the most of the land that God – acting through Scottish landowners – gave them. They employed labourers to pan for salt, make charcoal, drain marshy land and extract coal. Such knowledge soon spread. With more money to sustain them, their churches and monasteries – such as the great border abbeys at Melrose, Jedburgh, Kelso and Dryburgh, as well as Inchaffray in Perthshire, which was built in a swamp – were bigger, taller and longer-lasting than much of what had gone before. Inside, the walls were richly decorated with saints and bible stories to impress and educate a largely illiterate congregation.

And the increasing wealth produced by the Church and the nobility alike had a new outlet in the burghs, also introduced by David I. Though towns existed before, especially in the east with easy access to rivers and the North Sea link to Europe, now the king made sure that they were consistently governed, had regular markets and fairs, and that taxes – called customs – were imposed and collected on what was traded, a significant boost to royal coffers. Craftspeople no longer tended to work in hill-top forts or other elite sites, including monasteries, but had their own quarters within the new burghs where they could more easily sell their wares to anyone who could afford them.

By the middle of the thirteenth century, then, Scotland had been transformed. Even the kingdom's identity had changed. After 1200, written documents no longer spoke of all the various peoples owing allegiance to Scotland's kings – Franks (Normans), Britons, Gaels, Saxons – nor the journeys from one part of their

Jedburgh Abbey, Borders
The Augustinian abbey at Jedburgh was built between 1118 and c1147, another of the great Border foundations of King David I. HES. Engraving from *Border Antiquities of England and Scotland* Volume II by Sir Walter Scott.

Dryburgh Abbey, Borders
Situated beside the River
Tweed, this abbey – like others
in the Borders – suffered during
periods of warfare between
Scotland and England. HES

domains to another, of which Scotland (Alba) was only one, with Moray, Strathclyde and the Lothians some of the others. Now Scotland meant the entirety of his possessions and the king was sensitive to any suggestion that he was not the ultimate authority within his kingdom, but subject to the power of another, namely the king of England.

This was an old story. Scottish attempts to move the border further into Northumbrian territory ended in military disaster and solemn promises to be loyal to England's kings through the swearing of homage and fealty, promises that were swiftly broken. By the mid-thirteenth century, both rulers agreed the border was now fixed and the Scottish king was rewarded with lucrative English lands. But when he and his successors went to swear homage and fealty for those lands in England (as they had to do for every new English king), they were asked to make the same oath for the kingdom of Scotland too. This they would not countenance.

In reality, the two royal families were closely allied, Alexander III (1249–86) of Scotland having married Margaret, daughter of Henry III of England. As an assertive, effective king, Alexander did not fear England. But he should have feared biology, for the downside of primogeniture was about to hit Scotland with a vengeance.

CHAPTER FOUR
A TIME OF CONFLICT 1286–1371

War with England was the last thing Scotland's nobles expected after the sudden death of King Alexander III, who fell from his horse to his death one stormy March night in 1286 without a male heir to succeed him. The relationship between the neighbouring kingdoms had grown increasingly close over the previous fifty years after Scottish kings were given English lands in return for promising to stop trying to push the border further south into Northumberland. No, what preyed on the minds of Scotland's leaders was the very real threat of a civil war launched by the wily old lord of Annandale, Robert Bruce, who now claimed to have been named heir to the dead king's father before Alexander III had been born.

So, to begin with, the English king, Edward I, was seen as a friend in Scotland's hour of need. The marriage of Alexander's granddaughter and heir, Margaret, Maid of Norway, to Edward's only surviving son, was eagerly sought by both sides. But after the little Maid's death in 1290, the English king seized the opportunity to turn ancient but fairly nebulous claims of overlordship into very real power over John Balliol, the man judged by Edward's court to be the

King Robert Bruce This statue by Charles Pilkington Jackson was installed at the Bannockburn Heritage Centre near the site of Bruce's famous victory. HES

rightful heir to Scotland's throne in 1292. Despite later propaganda by the Bruces, who thought they should have been given the crown, most Scottish nobles agreed with the English king that Balliol should succeed Alexander III.

What is remarkable, then, is not that Edward I should have made very strident claims of overlordship, but that Scotland's leaders refused to accept the unprecedented power he then asserted over the new king. Though many of them had family and lands in Anglo-Norman England, some were equally at home in the very different Gaelic world out of which the kingdom of Scotland had sprung. For almost all of them, Scotland's distinctive political landscape and histories of ancient independence, however manufactured, were too ingrained to be cast aside without a fight.

It helped, too, that they could ally with France, with whom Edward was about to go to war. But in a matter of weeks in 1296, the English king and his army defeated the Scots in battle, dethroned John Balliol and set up direct rule – much to the dismay of the Bruce family, who thought it was their turn. But if Edward I of England's decision to end decades of peace by attempting to absorb Scotland into his domains was a shock,

Siege of Bothwell Castle
This impressive castle on the River Clyde was besieged and taken by Edward I of England in 1301. The Scots got it back in 1314. HES

John Balliol
Chosen to become Scottish king in 1292, Balliol was no match for Edward I, who made unprecedented demands of him as overlord of Scotland. Licensor Scran. From the Forman Armorial manuscript, c1562.

he was only doing what kings and nobles were supposed to do in acquiring more territory. Scotland itself had expanded well beyond its original boundaries, usually by conquest, though the Hebrides and the Isle of Man had been acquired from the Norwegians by negotiation as recently as 1266, following many years of Scottish campaigning.

But 1296 was just the beginning. What followed was nearly half a century of bitter fighting and over 350 years of intermittent warfare. This terrible conflict not only fundamentally changed the relationship between Scotland and England, it altered the political geography of the northern kingdom and reshaped the identity of the Scots.

But first Scotland's commanders had to learn how to fight more effectively, which meant largely avoiding set-piece battles focused on the unstoppable charge of mounted knights, the stuff of chivalry and what nobles, whether Scottish or English, had trained to do since childhood. Using guerrilla tactics was eminently sensible, given the numbers and resources that English kings had at their disposal compared to the Scottish leaders, who relied on much smaller armies largely made up of footsoldiers with spears rather than cavalry. Scotland's rough terrain and sheer size also made it possible for small, mobile forces to isolate and surprise English garrisons or even small English armies. English morale and resources were also dwindling after many decades of war in Wales, Scotland and on the Continent.

With John Balliol in exile from 1296, the Scottish political community also showed great resilience in waging war without a king, choosing Guardians to lead the nation in battle and diplomacy, as they had done after King Alexander's death. The most famous of these was William Wallace, who, along with Andrew Murray, defeated an English army at Stirling Bridge, but also went on diplomatic missions to France and probably Rome and Norway. With the exception of Wallace, however, Scottish resistance to Edward I was hampered by the great fissure between those nobles who supported the Bruce claim to the throne – represented now by the grandson of the man who lost to Balliol in 1292, yet another Robert Bruce – and those who remained loyal to the absent Balliol. This issue was settled, temporarily at least, when Bruce returned to the English side in late 1301.

Edward I
A formidably competent English king who fought many wars, Edward found that, though Scotland might be conquered, it was fiendishly difficult to hold for long. Copyright Hunterian Museum. Licensor Scran. Early long cross penny depicting Edward I.

Stirling Castle
Many battles were fought in
the area around Stirling Castle,
including the Scottish victory at
Stirling Bridge in 1297.
HES DP079016

Scotland's History

Balliol's cause was led by Scotland's most powerful family, the Comyns. As a Scottish Guardian between 1298 and 1304, John Comyn of Badenoch was a tried and tested war leader. He was also nephew of John Balliol, who had sailed from England into papal custody in France in 1299 while Pope Boniface VIII considered whether or not to examine the legality of the English king's actions in taking over Scotland. In 1301 Balliol was passed over to the French king, which both Edward I and the Scots thought was the prelude to the Scottish king's return at the head of a French army. But by late 1302 Philip IV of France wanted to make peace with Edward I so he could concentrate on his own territorial ambitions in Flanders (part of modern Belgium), leaving the Scots in the lurch. In 1303 John Balliol renounced his claim to the Scottish throne to Philip IV and lived the rest of his life on his French estates in Picardy until his death in 1314.

Despite this diplomatic isolation, John Comyn continued to fight. But when Edward I managed to keep an army in Scotland over the winter of 1303–4, Comyn decided to sue for peace on behalf of all those Scots still fighting against the English. This was a chance to recover from eight years of war, but the Scots were surely waiting

Wallace versus Bruce – A war of liberation is often led by a hero, but Scotland managed to produce more than one – although neither is quite what their reputations suggest. While Sir William Wallace was no great nobleman, he wasn't a peasant either, but the younger son of a small landowner. And though he did use scorched-earth tactics in 1298 to starve out the English army after his victory at Stirling Bridge in 1297 – won alongside another young commander, Andrew Murray – he then abandoned guerrilla tactics and lost a set-piece battle at Falkirk. But he was fiercely committed to the fight for independence and despised noble politics. Perhaps that was why, when the Scots sued for peace in 1304, Wallace alone paid the price for Edward I's desire for vengeance. His terrible death became a martyrdom and his largely unknown life a blank sheet for stories and legends to fill. Later writers even imagined him persuading Robert Bruce to abandon King Edward to fight for Scottish independence. In truth, Bruce was only interested in his own ambitions. Brought up to believe his family had been robbed of the crown, he had plotted to wear it since he was a teenager, changing sides when it suited. But when he finally seized the throne in 1306, he proved an inept commander. Forced out of the country with many of his own people set against him, Bruce returned as a master of guerrilla tactics. He also brought new techniques to give his infantry army the edge over mounted cavalry on the rare occasions he felt the need to give battle, most particularly at Bannockburn in 1314. Destroying his own castles so that they would not fall into enemy hands, he was more than a match for Edward II. But despite throwing everything at the English king, including an invasion of Ireland, Bruce could not get him to accept his kingship and Scotland's independence. It was only by exploiting English unrest after Edward II's deposition and murder, which led to the Treaty of Northampton–Edinburgh in 1328, that King Robert could finally take off his spurs. He died a year later; his heart was taken in a casket by his great friend and comrade, James Douglas, on 'crusade' against the Moors in Spain. The peace lasted only four short years.

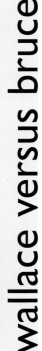

Robert Bruce
Fighting against England and many Scots, Bruce became a military commander of genius, though he generally avoided battles, preferring guerrilla tactics. HES. Statue at Edinburgh Castle.

William Wallace
Single-minded and charismatic, Wallace was deeply committed to the cause of Scottish independence and paid for it with his life in 1305. HES. Statue at Edinburgh Castle.

for the death of the ailing English king before naming a new leader and starting the conflict all over again. With John Balliol's son Edward still in English custody, Comyn seems to have intended to take the throne himself – until he was murdered by Robert Bruce in February 1306.

The wars between Scotland and England came at a bad time. As the climate grew colder and wetter, harvests failed, while cattle and sheep diseases decimated the herds. People would have starved without the added distress of armies marching over their land and destroying – or taking – whatever they could find.

Edward I died in July 1307 and was succeeded by his son, Edward II. Inheriting an almost empty treasury, the new English king soon gained a reputation for extravagance, which many of his nobles sought to rein in. Though Edward II wanted to prosecute the war in Scotland, he did not like having to ask parliament for money for men and supplies in case he was forced to cut back on other expenditure. North-east England fared worst, with many places deserted thanks to systematic Scottish raids and the English king's neglect.

But south-east Scotland – often English-held and the main route for English armies coming

Edward II

Inheriting his father's copious debts, Edward proved a weak and divisive king, losing at Bannockburn to Bruce who 'sent him homeward tae think again'. Lebrecht History / Bridgeman Images. Portrait from *History of England*, Vol 1 by Hume and Smollett.

north – fared almost as badly. King Robert was cautious about granting away his enemies' Scottish lands to his allies, partly because he hoped some of them would return to support him. It was only towards the end of his reign that he granted out more, with a number of supporters from the south-east receiving lands some distance away from the war zone.

The biggest beneficiaries from this policy in the long run were the Douglases. Originally from south-west Scotland, James Douglas defended the eastern border for King Robert and was well rewarded with lands and other property there. In 1358, his nephew became earl of Douglas and the family continued to acquire property and influence, becoming some of the most powerful nobles in the land, whose great wealth and power brought them into conflict with King James II. Worried that his own authority was compromised by such an overmighty subject, James murdered the eighth earl and forfeited the rest of the family in spectacular fashion in the 1450s.

The wars with England not only redrew the political map within Scotland in terms of those who lost and gained lands, but also began the shift in power away from the core Scottish kingdom north of the River Forth towards the border with England. Though Scottish kings still spent time in 'Alba' and some were well-versed in Gaelic culture, the Gaelic language was in retreat from 1300. Even before the outbreak of war, commentators in the Lowlands were keen to stress the differences – largely in their favour as law-abiding, settled farmers – between them and cattle-rearing, lawless Highlanders.

Certainly Hebridean noblemen in particular, with their close ties to Ireland and Norse–Gaelic inheritance, continued to live by long-standing warrior customs, selling their swords as gallowglass (*gall óglaigh*: foreign warriors) and demanding protection money from neighbouring communities. But the wars also encouraged southern noblemen to keep armed retinues that did nothing to promote good justice.

King Robert had begun to address such problems of lawlessness before his death in 1329 when he was succeeded by his five-year old son, David. However, the renewal of war in 1332 threw the kingdom into the grip of factions once more. It was instigated by the arrival of Edward Balliol (son of King John) who came north with the unofficial support of Edward III of England and an army of Disinherited – those who had lost

David II and Edward III

Though Robert Bruce secured a peace treaty with England, war broke out again in the reign of his son David II, this time against Edward III. Detail from fourteenth-century Cotton Nero D VI manuscript.

their Scottish lands for opposing King Robert. By September 1332, Scotland had two kings, though in the spring of 1334 David II was sent to France for safety.

Without the older generation of commanders, the Scots forgot the military lessons they had learned, especially how to use tactics appropriate to different battlefields. But the English had absorbed these lessons, now using archers to inflict damage at a distance rather than relying on cavalry charges. However, Edward Balliol was a poor leader and a series of Guardians for David II held their ground, despite a series of terrible defeats once Edward III began to intervene directly from 1333. However, the English king was, like his grandfather, soon embroiled in disputes with Scotland's ally, France, and in 1338 Edward III agreed to a truce with the Scots so that he could concentrate on regaining his French possessions.

David II returned to Scotland in 1341 but was captured during an invasion of England in 1346. However, the Scots refused to bargain for his release at the cost of naming King Edward III or one of his sons as heir. A ransom was finally agreed and the Scottish king came home in 1357. England never again made a concerted effort to

Archer from fourteenth-century manuscript
The success of Robert Bruce's footsoldiers against English mounted knights led Edward III and his successors to foster the skills of English and Welsh archers. Copyright British Library Board. All Rights Reserved / Bridgeman Images. Detail from the Luttrell Psalter manuscript, c1330.

conquer the northern kingdom, but campaigns and invasions were always a possibility for both sides. And now the Scots rejoiced in a European reputation as tough fighters who had seen off, and always would see off, the Auld Enemy, their kingdom (unlike England) '1,600 years unconquered'.

CHAPTER FIVE
RECOVERY 1371–1542

After half a century of war (from 1296 to 1346) that often pitched families, friends and neighbours against one another, saw fortunes made or lost almost overnight, disrupted agricultural cycles, interrupted trade, and caused misery to countless men, women and children whose voices have largely been silenced, Scotland needed to recover.

But it would not be easy. Since 1286, the power of the monarchy had been weakened by vacancy, absence and violent usurpation. Then, in 1371, David II died without children and was succeeded by his nephew, Robert Stewart. Robert had not only been David's heir, but often an alternative power in the land, especially during the king's absences. As the first of a new dynasty, Robert II faced his own troubles, mostly arising from within his own family, including the MacDonald Lords of the Isles, aided and abetted by other powerful nobles such as the earls of Douglas. It was not until the middle of the fifteenth century that Stewart kings successfully began to curb the power of their mightiest subjects, and even then they were still content to leave much of the administration of justice and decision-making to their nobility at a local level.

Stirling Castle Perched on a rocky outcrop above the River Forth, this strategic site controlled the all-important north–south river crossing. There has probably been a fortification here since prehistoric times. HES

Nevertheless the Scottish state expanded despite, and sometimes because of, these tensions. From the mid-fourteenth century, parliament's structure and role became formalised with representatives of the Church, the Nobility and the Burghs. These Three Estates sat where and when necessary to approve, among other things, land grants, taxation and royal legislation that, as late as 1398, still had to take action against 'great and horrible destructions' caused by gangs of armed men, a hangover from the conflict with England, which still occasionally broke out into open warfare. Royal justice – concerned with the most heinous crimes – moved around the country too, with the king himself sometimes presiding over a system of government that still prized the personal touch. It was not until 1532 that a central law court was established in Edinburgh.

But war and its repercussions were not the worst aspects of the fourteenth century. The Black Death arrived in 1349, its various recurring strains killing between a quarter and a third of Scots, mostly in the south and east, where ports connected the kingdom to Europe and England. The population was already in

The Black Death
The bubonic plague arrived in Europe in 1347 on an Italian ship fleeing attack. It spread rapidly, killing up to 60 per cent of Europe's inhabitants – some 50 million people. Bridgeman Images. Fourteenth-century engraving.

decline thanks to the poorer climate so, for those who survived, wages almost certainly increased even as the cost of basic necessities may have gone down. Landowners no longer had their pick of labour, which probably explains the disappearance of serfs – peasants bound to their lord's estate – rather than any sentiment about freedom pervading Scottish writings about the war with England.

And though Scottish noblemen did not try to use legislation to keep down wages (as they did in England, leading to the Peasants' Revolt of 1381), they demanded action against social inferiors with more money in their pockets who dared to go around dressed in silk and other luxury cloths throughout the fifteenth century. Plain wool, leather and linen – made into the kinds of tunics, dresses, shoes and jackets commonly worn by peasants and craftspeople across Western Europe – were considered to be good enough for them.

But with fewer people to buy products across Europe, the Scottish wool trade – which has been compared to oil in the twentieth century – was struck particularly hard. Before the outbreak of the wars with England, Scottish fleeces had been in high demand, especially from Flemish cloth manufacturers, and often bought years in advance. But though the Scots used Bruges in Flanders as their 'staple' (monopoly) port until 1477, their wool was by then being side-lined as too coarse for the fine cloth that might have made up for the decline in purchases of cheap fabric. Given that the Scottish Crown derived much of its income from the customs on wool, it is no wonder that parliament kept a close eye on it.

As ever, economic fortunes fluctuate and there are always winners and losers. Scotland had more raw materials than just wool and, from coal to timber to fish, these were sent increasingly to England from the later fifteenth century, as well as to other parts of Europe, bringing wealth to landowners and merchants. At the same time, the peasantry were beginning to feel the squeeze as rents rose along with the price of goods. Among the upper classes there were certainly plenty of Scots with money to spend, as demonstrated by the great castles such as those of the Douglas family at Tantallon and Threave, royal palaces at Linlithgow and Falkland, cathedrals at St Andrews, Aberdeen and Dunkeld, and tower houses such as at the bishop of Moray's palace at Spynie.

For the overwhelming majority of people, houses were generally flimsy, but easily put up and rebuilt with materials found close at hand. Wattle-and-daub walls – wooden strips held together with a mixture of wet soil, straw and dung – were no doubt common, but turf was surely also used, together with thatched roofs of straw or reeds. Houses tended to be built low to the ground to combat the prevailing westerly winds and had a section in which to keep animals during the winter, all of which helped to preserve warmth where it might be found. These homes were probably little different from those built for many centuries before and would linger for many centuries to come.

Such houses were likely to have been common in towns as well, but more substantial structures made out of timber (and some stone), with protruding upper stories, added to the perennial danger of fire in the tightly-packed streets. This was another issue on which king and parliament often had an opinion, banning the unhappy combination of hay and candles in preference for lanterns in 1427.

On the international stage, Scotland continued to be seen as small and even backward – the future Pope Pius II, Aeneas Silvius Piccolomini,

Tantallon Castle, East Lothian
Defended by sea cliffs, the great sandstone castle built by the formidable Douglas family eventually proved vulnerable to cannon fire and was surrendered to King James V in 1529. HES

Linlithgow Palace,
West Lothian

Originally a royal hunting
lodge, by the sixteenth century
Linlithgow was transformed
into a magnificent palace fit for
the increasingly powerful kings
of Scots. HES DP101766. Copy
of engraving titled 'Prospectus
Regis Palatis Limnuchensis'.

who visited in 1435, dismissed the kingdom as of no consequence, rude, uncultivated, and unvisited by the winter sun. Although Scotland failed to find favour with Piccolomini, his remarks contrast with clear evidence in the later Middle Ages for sophisticated architectural accomplishments such as the sculptures adorning Linlithgow Palace and the flowering of Scottish literature, including poets like Robert Henryson, William Dunbar and Gavin Douglas. While there had been music in Scotland from the earliest times, to judge from the remains of ancient instruments and those portrayed on Pictish stones, from the later fifteenth century Scotland entered a golden age that reached new heights with the composer Robert Carver (c1485–c1570). And, to temper Piccolomini's remarks still further, while fourteenth-century Scottish monarchs had been preoccupied with British affairs and tended to marry local women, their fifteenth-century successors proved able to take advantage of European politics. This was often, but not exclusively, as a proven antidote to the English, especially in the latter's continuing quarrels with France.

The third Stewart monarch, James I (1406–37), played his cards well during a papal schism, getting permission from one of the competing popes to establish Scotland's first university at St Andrews in 1413. Then James II (1437–60) received an enormous sum of money on his marriage to Mary of Gueldres, great-niece of the powerful Duke of Burgundy, in 1449. His son, James III (1460–88), acquired the islands of Orkney and Shetland – putting the finishing touches to Scotland's boundaries – when he married Margaret of Denmark. The marriage of James IV (1488–1513) to Margaret Tudor – sister of Henry VIII of England – in 1503 was supposed to mark the beginning of a Perpetual Peace between the warring kingdoms (even if James did invade England at France's behest only ten years later).

The biggest winner in the diplomatic stakes was undoubtedly James V (1513–42). Courted by the pope and Catholic France as Henry VIII plunged England into Protestantism, he was amply rewarded with marriage to a French princess and, after her death, a second French wife from the powerful Guise family. With Mary of Guise at his side, James initiated a major refurbishment of the royal apartments at Stirling

Fountain, Linlithgow Palace courtyard
This sixteenth-century fountain is topped by an imperial crown, while on the surrounding walls animals and human figures spy on unsuspecting visitors. HES

IACOBVS, QVINTVS, SCOTTORVM REX &

James V

Perhaps Scotland's most politically astute monarch, James died aged thirty in 1542. On learning of his daughter Mary's birth a week earlier, he did not think his dynasty would survive. He was wrong. Copyright Mark Fiennes Archive / Bridgeman Images. Copy of the original double portrait of Mary of Guise and James V commissioned by Lord Bute, 1895.

Mary of Guise
James V's second wife arranged her daughter Mary's French upbringing and marriage. She became regent of Scotland in 1554 and died in 1560 on the eve of the Protestant Reformation.
Copyright Mark Fiennes Archive / Bridgeman Images. Copy of the original double portrait of Mary of Guise and James V commissioned by Lord Bute, 1895.

MARIA, LOTHORINGIA, ILLIVS, IN, SECVNDIS, N

Castle in the 1530s along the lines of a French chateau. Though he did not live to see it, this became the first Renaissance palace in Britain, with a series of complementary 'his and hers' royal rooms sumptuously decorated with ornate furniture, as well as the wooden carvings known as the Stirling Heads, richly painted walls and enormous tapestries.

Like so many of his predecessors stretching back beyond the formation of Scotland itself, James V loved to hunt. Even in the sixteenth century, hunting offered aristocrats a pastime that honed physical prowess at a time when kings and nobles were still expected to lead in war. Indeed, James's own father had been killed fighting the English at Flodden in 1513, the last king in Britain to die in battle.

Hunting also gave kings and nobles the opportunity to show off. This was certainly the intention when James V and his mother, Margaret Tudor, were invited to a spectacular hunt organised by the earl of Atholl in the moors above Glen Tilt in the 1530s. To house the assembled dignitaries over three days, a temporary palace was built out of wood, complete with glass windows, tapestries and silk hangings. The whole shebang, including all the

Unicorn, Stirling Castle tapestry

The unicorn, a symbol of purity and fertility, was particularly associated with Scotland's kings and was adopted into their coat of arms in the sixteenth century.
HES

food, cost £1,000 (over half a million now) and quite astonished the papal ambassador, who never imagined he would see such a thing in 'The Arse of the World'.

It is not clear whether the ambassador's disparaging comment described Scotland as a whole or the Highlands – where the hunt took place – in particular. Certainly King James was said to have remarked, as the wooden 'palace' was put to the flames on their departure, that this was a Highland habit, no matter how substantial the lodging, as if to suggest both wealth and profligacy in a region renowned – in the Lowlands – for the second but not the first.

The culture clash between Gaels and Lowland Scots had existed since at least the thirteenth century. By the mid-sixteenth century Highlanders were called 'wild Scottish' by their Lowland contemporaries, adept at dealing with animals for the hunt but otherwise not fit for 'civilised' company. The power of the MacDonald Lords of the Isles had been summarily smashed by the king at the end of the fifteenth century. This is not to say that the Highlands immediately fell under effective royal control. The power vacuum that followed the removal of the Lords of the Isles, along with an enduring martial and kin-based culture, was ripe for exploitation by other Highland families, most notably the Campbells of Argyll and later the Mackenzies of Kintail, both of whom acted as Crown agents.

The MacDonald Lords of the Isles – The MacDonalds were descendants of Somerled, a twelfth-century *Rí Innse* Gall (King of the Isles). Based on Islay with their main residence at Finlaggen, like many Hebridean families they had both Norse and Celtic blood. The MacDonalds became the most important family in the west by supporting King Robert I, while their rivals, the Macdougalls, lost out for opposing him. John, the first Lord of the Isles (since they acknowledged the power of the kings of Scots, they could not be kings themselves), married Margaret, daughter of the first Stewart king, Robert II, who was himself part of the Gaelic world as lord of Bute. The Hebrides had only come into the possession of Scottish kings in 1266, and the wars with England prevented them from fully integrating the islands into their kingdom. The Lords of the Isles took advantage of the lack of royal authority to expand their power to the mainland. They used their mastery of the seaways to maintain their authority across domains that stretched from Ireland's Glens of Antrim in the west to the outskirts of Aberdeen in the north-east. They also

Scotland's History

promoted Gaelic culture as patrons of bards, singers and musicians proficient in the clarsach (harp) and, from the fifteenth century, bagpipes.

It was the Lords of the Isles' claim to the earldom of Ross that brought them into direct conflict with the Scottish Crown. In 1411 Donald of the Isles was forced back to Islay after the battle of Harlaw near Inverurie. Though his successors kept the earldom throughout much of the fifteenth century, they over-reached themselves by signing a treaty with the English king, Edward IV, in 1462 during the Wars of the Roses. When Edward IV decided to make peace with the Scottish king James III, John, the last Lord of the Isles, lost his land and titles for his treachery. Even though he regained his Hebridean possessions in 1476, he lost the earldom of Ross and other mainland possessions and with it much of his prestige and authority. Unable to control his own family, John was finally forfeited in 1493. Despite attempts to restore the Lordship of the Isles and much poetry, song and stories lamenting its demise, MacDonald power was finished in Scotland.

Highland galley
The West Highland galley or *birlinn* was probably Norse in origin and played a fundamental role in trade, diplomacy, warfare and cultural connections for nobles like the Lords of the Isles.
HES SC940894. Carving from the tomb of Alexander Macleod, c1528.

CHAPTER SIX
MARY, QUEEN OF SCOTS, AND THE PROTESTANT AGE 1542–1603

The medieval Church was like an interfering but potentially useful neighbour to most Scots, the sound of its bells – set atop what were often the only stone buildings for miles around – uniting town and countryside. Its doctrines and activities affected everyone's lives in so many ways, from marking birth, death and marriage to looking after the destitute, from providing education to well-off children and future clergy to advising kings and writing the nation's history in strident nationalistic tones. It was the Church that decided which days were holidays (literally, holy days) and when meat could be eaten, though this was less relevant to Scottish peasants, who couldn't afford much of it anyway.

The Church was, of course, an international organisation with the shrewdness and political clout of any big business. In Scotland, as elsewhere, it owned a considerable amount of land, gifted by kings and nobles in return for prayers for their souls. The great Border abbeys – Kelso, Jedburgh, Dryburgh, Melrose – grazed enormous numbers of small native sheep

Mary, Queen of Scots Mary was a Catholic queen of Protestant Scotland. Preachers like John Knox often spoke out against her. Bridgeman Images. Oil painting by Samuel Sidley, 1874.

across the nearby Southern Uplands. They made fortunes out of the wool trade until its terminal decline in the sixteenth century, but also suffered from the destruction caused by the wars with England.

For many Scots, the Mass – the central point of the Catholic ritual – was surely most mysterious. When they entered a small church and especially a great cathedral, they could watch the priest and his helpers with the precious symbols of their office only from beyond a screen. Even more inscrutable were the monasteries, often deliberately set apart from the hustle of everyday life, though the preaching orders – Franciscans and Dominicans – were much more visible as they went about towns giving sermons and begging for food.

And though they were excluded from the mysteries of the Mass, most Scots understood the basics of the Christian doctrine and worried about the afterlife and God's judgement. As members of the Catholic faithful, they could and did make their way to the great pilgrimage centres of the Christian world such as Rome (following in the footsteps of King Macbeth), Santiago de Compostela, and even the Holy Land, seeking healing, absolution and, ultimately,

Jedburgh Abbey, Borders
After the Reformation, a new parish church was built into the nave of Jedburgh Abbey.
HES

Dunfermline Abbey, Fife
This abbey is mainly associated with Margaret, mother of David I. As a royal saint, she was much venerated and many of her royal descendants were buried here. HES

salvation. Easily identifiable by their 'uniforms' (rough tunic and woollen cloak, broad-brimmed hat, water bottle, food bag and stout staff), they also wore pilgrim's badges to show they were allowed to be out on the road away from home or had piously completed an arduous journey.

But most would not venture so far afield. Individual churches with links to popular or important saints such as St Andrews, St Duthac's at Tain and St Ninian's Shrine at Whithorn in Galloway attracted visitors from across Britain seeking spiritual solace. Dunfermline Abbey had its very own royal saint in Margaret, wife of Malcolm III, who died in 1093. Canonised in 1249 she was duly reburied in a magnificent shrine at the east end of the church the following year. This was a considerable coup for Scotland and its royal family, but it was Dunfermline that came off best. For over three centuries it enjoyed the prestige and prosperity bestowed upon a pilgrimage centre. But that all came to an abrupt end in 1560.

The road to Protestantism was a long one and its destination by no means assured. Since many Scottish merchants were literate and traded in Europe, they were just as aware as the nobility of serious criticisms of the Catholic Church. These

St Ninian

Ninian's identity is much disputed, but there's no doubt that his shrine at Whithorn was a popular pilgrimage site. HES. Stained glass window at St Margaret's Chapel in Edinburgh Castle, added 1922.

arose most notably in the wake of the German monk Martin Luther's damning indictment of the selling of indulgences – the granting of exemptions for the punishment of certain sins in return for money. At the same time, general economic pressures such as the decline of the wool trade which had once made the abbeys so rich meant that those in senior positions as bishops or abbots – often illegitimate royal sons or members of the higher nobility – increasingly had to rent out church assets in order to pay for the upkeep of buildings and the salaries of church personnel. At the bottom of the pile, the parish priest and the parish church undoubtedly had to make do with less money, which attracted poorer-quality applicants and in turn led to accusations of ignorance and unworthiness.

Yet there is little to suggest that churches and monasteries were failing to provide for the spiritual needs of most Scots or that they were no longer seen as a good career path for either the wealthy or the brightest. By now Scotland had three universities (compared with England's two) at St Andrews, Glasgow and Aberdeen, where the curriculum was meant to promote orthodox religious understanding

Martin Luther
This former priest kickstarted the Protestant Reformation in western Europe with his critique of unscriptural church practices in his *Ninety-five Theses*. Hi-Story / Alamy. Engraving, 1830.

among those who would become the next generation of priests. But while the Scottish Church would not tolerate views that seriously challenged orthodoxy and did burn a number of heretics, including a former St Andrews student, Patrick Hamilton, in 1528, it also tried to address its own shortcomings. A catechism in Scots was even issued to less well-educated parish priests to help them give the right message to the faithful.

As is often the case, it was a combination of circumstances and personalities that brought revolution to the boil. The initial factors acting as a catalyst for change were Henry VIII's decision to turn England Protestant in 1532, followed by the death of James V of Scotland ten years later at the age of thirty. James left behind his six-day-old daughter Mary and the thorny problem – soon to be faced by England too – of how a deeply patriarchal society would cope with a female ruler.

James also left behind his widow, the formidable Mary of Guise, who was in no doubt that her daughter should marry into the royal family of her native France, even as Henry VIII determined that she should become the wife of *his* son and heir. After Henry's death in 1547,

Patrick Hamilton
Though the burning of heretics
was rare in Scotland, one of
the most famous Protestant
martyrs was St Andrews
student Patrick Hamilton,
who died at the stake in 1528.
Falkensteinfoto / Alamy.

it was Mary of Guise who prevailed, sending little Mary to France in 1548. However, the queen-mother had needed French troops in Scotland to counteract an English invasion earlier that same year, fuelling concerns among some Scottish nobles that their interests were being neglected.

Private belief and public politics began to align once Elizabeth I of England ascended the throne in 1558 and started to pay surreptitious 'pensions' to Scottish nobles with Protestant leanings. Mary of Guise, as Regent for her absent daughter, pursued a relatively lenient policy towards those dabbling in the new ideas and tolerated some reform so as not to push them further into England's arms. But it was hard to know what the future held once the fifteen-year-old queen of Scots married the heir to the French throne in April 1558. Just over a year later, in July 1559, Mary became queen of France as well as Scotland, but the role for which she had been groomed since childhood lasted only until her husband's death in December 1560.

Scotland's Protestant nobles soon tried to whip up revolt. However, basing their grievances on religious grounds proved difficult, so they focused on liberating the kingdom from unwarranted foreign interference, meaning France.

Mary, Queen of Scots: misguided or misjudged? – Much ink has been spilled on the subject of Queen Mary's reputation, but we should remember that she was never meant to come back to Scotland and was quite unschooled in most of the skills needed to rule. As the beautiful, cultivated consort to the French king, her role had been largely decorative. As ruler of Scotland she had a very different job.

So long as she relied on the advice of her half-brother, James, earl of Moray, the young Queen delighted her subjects and charmed many of her nobility, if not John Knox, who lambasted her from his pulpit. But in marrying her deeply unpleasant cousin, Henry, Lord Darnley, she united many factions against her.

Personally brave if rarely in control of events and often displaying poor judgement, Mary took the opposite view to her cousin Elizabeth of England on the issue of marriage. While Elizabeth sacrificed the chance of a direct heir for political independence, the Scottish queen's marriage unleashed perceptions of a power imbalance tilted in favour of her husband. Despite a brief moment of unity after the birth of her son James in 1566, the drift towards civil war became brutally relentless.

In early 1567 Darnley was murdered in Edinburgh. Suspicion fell on the man who would abduct and marry Mary a few months later – James Hepburn, earl of Bothwell. In taking the queen as his wife, he united all the factions against him *and* her. After defeat at Carberry Hill in June, Bothwell fled to Denmark, later dying in prison. Mary was taken to the island fortress in Loch Leven, where she miscarried twins and was forced to abdicate. Escaping in May 1568, the queen rallied her troops, but fled to England after yet another defeat at the

Battle of Langside against forces led by the Earl of Moray.

In the end, there was no way back for Mary once she had thrown herself on the mercy of Queen Elizabeth in 1568. Elizabeth had no choice but to imprison the woman who had long claimed her throne by virtue of being Catholic. Mary's execution in 1587 after nearly twenty years in captivity made her a martyr as much as William Wallace, ensuring that her story – like his – will never lose its appeal.

Execution of Mary, Queen of Scots

Mary's tragic and dramatic end in 1587 sealed her fate as a romantic historical figure who still inspires films and books today. Classic Image / Alamy. From *The National and Domestic History of England* by William Aubrey, c1890.

mary, queen of scots

Queen Elizabeth I

Cousin of the Scottish queen, Elizabeth was well aware that Mary both claimed her throne and was a potential heir so long as she remained childless. Copyright National Portrait Gallery. The 'Darnley portrait' by an unknown artist, c1575.

Mary, Queen of Scots
Though Mary undoubtedly
faced many problems
presiding over a profoundly
misogynist society, she was
not as well-equipped to deal
with her role as Elizabeth.
Copyright National Portrait
Gallery. Portrait after
Nicholas Hilliard.

Side-lining Mary of Guise, the Protestant lords formed a new government and agreed a treaty with England, even though they still vowed allegiance to Queen Mary. In August 1560 parliament met and abolished the Mass and the power of the Pope. Scotland was now officially Protestant, though its monarch was not.

Given the generally sad state of decay of pre-Reformation buildings in Scotland today, from chapels and shrines to great cathedrals, it is tempting to imagine that this was a period of great upheaval with churches and their treasures destroyed. But in fact, with the exception of a few violent incidents and more widespread looting, this was a far less calamitous affair than the Reformation in England or the counter-Reformation in France. In many cases, the Catholic clergy simply became ministers of the new Church or, if they were monks, were allowed to live out their lives in peace.

Nor did Protestantism establish itself throughout the kingdom overnight, though some of the east-coast towns such as Dundee and St Andrews quickly brought in ministers and appointed kirk sessions to manage parish affairs, both spiritual and temporal.

The Highlands were not neglected, but most ministers did not speak Gaelic, which made it difficult to ground the new religion effectively, while Catholicism proved hard to shift in the north-east too.

Many of the new Church's problems stemmed from a lack of money, which hastened the demise of a number of great medieval cathedrals and abbeys left to decay. One of the most laudable aims of the Scottish Reformation – which was heavily influenced by the French theologian John Calvin as interpreted by prominent Scottish preachers like John Knox – was that the number of schools should be increased until there was one in every parish. Given that Protestantism stressed the role of the individual – rather than the priest – in salvation, being able to read the bible in one's own language was extremely important. Unfortunately, the government was less keen on handing over enough of the assets confiscated from the Catholic Church to pay for salaries, the upkeep of existing buildings and the founding of new schools across the country. But there is no doubt that, despite continuing economic difficulties, literacy rates soon improved dramatically across the social spectrum.

John Knox
Knox, who had suffered for his beliefs before the Scottish Reformation, played a key role in establishing Protestantism in Scotland. HES. Statue in St Giles Cathedral, Edinburgh.

Lochleven Castle

Set in the middle of a loch, this castle looks impregnable. Yet in 1568 Queen Mary escaped, although it didn't do her much good in the end.
HES

As well as sweeping away nearly a millennium of religious uniformity shared with the rest of Western Europe, the Reformation also marked a decisive shift away from the comfort of the Auld Alliance with France in favour of a rapprochement with England. Given that the last English invasion was as recent as 1547, this was a major turn-around that would have a profound effect on the history of the British Isles. But in turning away from old conflicts, the potential to unleash new ones based on the logic of new beliefs soon became evident.

CHAPTER SEVEN
ABSENTEE KINGS AND THE ROCKY ROAD TO UNION 1603–1700

In April 1603 King James VI hotfooted it down to London to become James I of England on the death of Queen Elizabeth, whose aunt, Margaret Tudor, had married James's great-grandfather, James IV of Scotland. This was the Union of the Crowns, though both kingdoms were governed independently of each other. James promised to return to his homeland regularly, but actually managed it only once, an issue of some importance in a kingdom where the personal relationships the monarch cultivated with the governing classes did much to steady the ship of state.

James prided himself on his ability to rule Scotland from a distance, but at the time of his death twenty-two years later, the knotty problems that were rearing their heads even before he left for England had become more entrenched. The main disputes were profoundly interlinked, encompassing contradictory views on the nature of the individual's relationship to God and a sovereign's relationship with his people.

Having challenged the Catholic Church's monopoly in interpreting the Bible, the Protestant Church now found its own

James VI examines North Berwick witches James had a scholarly interest in witchcraft, though less so by the time he succeeded Elizabeth to become James I of England in 1603. Bridgeman Images. Engraving from *Newes from Scotland*, 1591.

doctrines subject to different interpretations. Scotland's reformers, taking the lead from European thinkers, especially John Calvin, intended the new church to be Presbyterian in outlook and organisation. Emphasising God's sovereignty, the supremacy of the scriptures and the importance of grace through faith, it was profoundly egalitarian, so long as you were a man. Every parish was supposed to be subject to the discipline of the minister, supported by a kirk session of local worthies called Elders; their representatives met regularly at a national level in the General Assembly.

Despite the best efforts of those who taught him as a boy, King James profoundly disliked such egalitarian principles, far preferring the hierarchical structure of the Episcopal (from the Latin word for bishops) version of Protestantism that prevailed in England. The desire to see Presbyterianism accepted as Scotland's national religion was to become a matter of life and death in the seventeenth century and to define Scottish identity for many centuries to come.

The loss of the monarch also had a profound effect on Scotland's capital, which was by far the kingdom's biggest town. Edinburgh had its non-native admirers then as now, but its biggest

Edinburgh, 1647
The city was bursting at its medieval seams –
St Giles' Cathedral (top) and Greyfriars Kirk (bottom left) stand out among the high-rise houses. HES DP101340. Detail of 'Bird's eye view of Edinburgh' by James Gordon of Rothemay.

Falkland Palace, Fife
Once a favoured royal residence, Falkland, like many another castle or palace, suffered neglect once the king relocated to England.
Iain Masterton / Alamy.

problem was the fact that it was still hemmed in by its medieval walls. This forced residents to build ever higher, duchesses living in the same tenements as goldsmiths and butchers. Though the palace at Holyrood, as with other royal residences such as Stirling Castle and Falkland Palace in Fife, were kept in a basic state of repair, it was not the same as when the court – which could number up to 600 persons – had been in regular residence. This had a knock-on effect on a wealth of entertainers, suppliers, not to mention staff and casual workers, required to keep them all fed, watered and amused. Native artistic endeavour now relied on the patronage of noble families and wealthy merchants and lawyers rather than the Crown.

King James also developed a new perspective on his original Scottish realm from his vantage point in London, worrying about the lawlessness that prevailed in the Borders, with ancient traditions of family loyalties and cattle raiding. A throw-back to the wars with England, such tendencies had long been encouraged by Scotland's kings, but they were now surplus to requirements. As early as 1609, the Scottish parliament legislated against the 'barbarous cruelty, wickedness and incivility which by

James VI and I
James promised to return often to Scotland after the court moved to London, but came only once. HES

inveterate custom almost was become natural to many of the inhabitants thereof' though such 'savages' clearly operated under the protection of noblemen and 'others of good quality'.

It was the same story in the Highlands, largely a result of the Crown's longstanding failure to do much more than castigate, then ignore, a region it really didn't understand. By now the antipathy of Lowland Scots – of whom James was one – towards Gaelic society and culture was made explicit with the demand, also in 1609, that chiefs would send their eldest sons to be 'civilised' in Lowland schools. There they would be made to speak and write English under the tuition of good Protestants.

But while the king certainly disliked disorder, he had other motives too. For he realised – thanks to the new access to English markets and English capital – that there were raw materials in the Highlands ready for exploitation and which, as parliament succinctly pointed out in 1609, 'by reason of the savageness of the inhabitants thereabouts were either unknown or at the least unprofitable and unused'. From timber and charcoal to iron-smelting and fishing, there were many who now sniffed opportunity in the Highlands. So far as the government was concerned, 'civilising' Protestantism was coming, whether the locals liked it or not, and with it the unruly momentum of commerce.

Many of the nobility had done well out of the Reformation, picking up lands, property and income that had once belonged to the Church. And when James became king of England, opportunities for lucrative patronage increased, though so too did the risk of significant debt as a consequence of the expense of English noble life. Slowly but surely a select group of wealthy and powerful aristocrats at the heart of government in both Edinburgh and London began to rise above the rest.

For everyone else, the most enduring sign of change was the degree of social control now exerted by the new Church's officers, who viewed individual behaviour of all kinds as very much their business. But they were particularly interested in sex and extreme poverty, defining much more closely what was and was not acceptable and dividing the destitute into deserving and undeserving.

It was women who came off particularly badly at a time when the opportunities for labourers were becoming scarcer. As ever, this is not a story of slow but incremental progress towards

Witch Hunting – Witchcraft has ancient origins, but making a pact with the Devil had worried the Catholic Church since the fifteenth century, mostly in connection with heresy (beliefs considered to be against Church teaching). The Scottish reformers explicitly vowed to destroy the works of the Devil and in 1567 the Scottish parliament legislated to make sure that witches – who explicitly did the Devil's work – were pursued and punished, threatening death even to those who consulted them. What constituted the Devil's work was, of course, a moot point, but it had moved well beyond questions of theology into everyday realms of folk medicine and evolving perceptions of acceptable behaviour.

The 1590s were a peak decade for witch hunting, during which James VI himself presided over a notorious trial. He had a personal interest in the case, since the accused – a supposed coven of witches from North Berwick – were reported to have conjured up a storm to sink the ship carrying the king and his new bride, Anna of Denmark. The plot was 'discovered' after the arrest and torture of a young servant girl, Gellie Duncan, for suspicious healing cures. It soon encompassed about 70 people, including the local schoolmaster, John Fian, a respected midwife, Agnes Sampson, and – unusually – the extremely high-born Francis Stewart, earl of Bothwell, the king's cousin. Some, including Gellie Duncan and Agnes Sampson, were burned as witches and James included the case in his 1597 treatise on the subject, Daemonologie.

Further witch-hunting peaks occurred every twenty years or so in the next century, coinciding with famines, war, general unrest or political change with at least 3,837 people accused in total. And while the number of people burned or drowned as witches was nowhere near the 30,000 once claimed these local – but state sanctioned – killing sprees often took the lives of unconventional or marginalised women. Thankfully, by the 1650s local magistrates were becoming sceptical about the threat posed by witchcraft, though an act repealing laws against such practices was not passed until 1736, seven years after Janet Horne in Dornoch was the last person in Scotland to be burned as a witch.

Punishment for witchcraft
Though the impetus behind witch hunting was many and varied, those found guilty were often poor women on the margins of society. Bridgeman Images. Seventeenth-century engraving.

Signing the
National Covenant

An extraordinary revolution took place in 1638 with this document rejecting Charles I's attempts to impose an English style of worship on the Scots. Copyright Look and Learn / Bridgeman Images. Nineteenth century engraving from *Scottish Pictures* by Samuel Green.

our own enlightened times, but an ebb and flow for reasons that are not always clear. In the thirteenth and fourteenth centuries, the range of jobs that a woman could do – brewer, merchant, engineer – was astonishingly varied, despite the fact that this was a period of rising population and thus highly competitive. By the seventeenth century, Protestantism seems to have brought into sharper focus what was – and was not – socially acceptable for women to be involved in.

And though there is plenty of misogyny among earlier, medieval Scottish writers, as elsewhere, Protestantism also brought real danger to anyone who ignored more clearly defined moral, doctrinal and social norms. The creation of kirk sessions filled with local men gave those moved by jealousy, superstition or even just a desire to make sense of challenging times, a forum in which to make accusations that might produce a legally binding result. From the later sixteenth century, the most controversial 'crimes' to bedevil local communities related to witchcraft – and women made up the majority of the accused.

The issue of which kind of Protestantism should prevail in Scotland soon became a marker of national identity, pitting increasingly informed and assertive members of the faithful against an ever more distant monarch. James VI laid the groundwork with his demand that the trappings of Episcopalianism, including bishops, be adopted in Scotland. This was on top of his belief that, as a godly prince, he was subject to no earthly authority. But the personal relationships that endured from the time when he was the ruler of only Scotland helped to smooth over these difficulties.

But the problems did not go away. And in his son Charles I, a fondness for the more Catholic end of Episcopalianism, combined with an even more strident belief in the divine right of kings, soon led to friction. Royal demands that an English-style prayer book should be used north of the border brought matters to a head and a riot which broke out in St Giles' Cathedral in Edinburgh in 1637 led to the drawing up of a National Covenant the following year. Its signatories – largely an impressive array of nobles, gentry, burgesses and clergy – bound themselves to defend the true religion, meaning Presbyterianism, and to live godly lives.

War broke out in 1639, catching on in England and Ireland three years later. Though the catalysts for rebellion and the aims of their leaders were different in each of Charles's three kingdoms, in essence most were challenging the power of the king to dictate on what they saw as matters of conscience, not to mention salvation. In Scotland, the issue of the Anglicisation of religious practice was also deeply resented.

Nearly a century after the Reformation, those ministers and local worthies who policed the moral behaviour of their neighbours and social inferiors were perfectly capable of standing up for their beliefs to a king they scarcely knew and who seemed to have little understanding of, or interest in, them. As for the nobility who largely directed events, they were, as ever, acting to defend their own privileges. But in drawing up the Covenant, these nobles inadvertently unleashed a challenge to the very notion that they spoke for the nation as large numbers of 'ordinary' folk now became involved in politics for the first time.

It did not go well for the Covenanters, as those who acted in defence of the Covenant were called. When the English radicals led by Oliver Cromwell beheaded Charles I in 1649, they did not consult the Scots. But worse was to follow. Charles's son fled north and was crowned at Scone in 1651 – the Scots were still entirely loyal

Oliver Cromwell
The execution of
Charles I was followed by
conflict between the Scots
and Cromwell. Cromwell
invaded in 1650 and Scotland
was occupied until Charles
II's restoration in 1660. Photo
copyright Derek Bayes /
Bridgeman Images.
Portrait by Sir Peter Lely,
seventeenth century.

Charles I
As a believer in the divine right of kings and with tendencies towards Catholicism, Charles proved difficult to deal with, leading to a bloody civil war across his three kingdoms. Bridgeman Images. Portrait by Jan Mijtens, 1629.

to the Stuarts, even if the latter needed tutoring in godly ways. But Charles II soon had to flee to the Netherlands when Cromwell's army, which had come north in 1650, defeated the Covenanters. Scotland was finally conquered and absorbed into the English Commonwealth in 1652.

This was a profound shock, but even when Charles II was restored to his thrones in 1660 the Covenanters were not daunted by his insistence on Episcopalianism. Taking to the fields and hills to hear their ejected Presbyterian ministers, they soon faced government troops and a number were executed. It was only with the removal of Charles's brother and heir James VII and II from his thrones for similar Catholic and authoritarian tendencies to their father that the Scots finally extracted the binding promise of official Presbyterianism as the price of their acceptance of William of Orange, husband of James's daughter Mary, as king in 1689.

It had been a hard and transformative century, underpinned by an admirable attempt to extend education more widely. There were shifting opportunities too as some of the rural population began to move into the towns, even from the Highlands in the summer months, bringing

Execution, believed to be Charles I

After Charles I surrendered to the Scots, they negotiated his hand-over to the English parliament. He was executed in January 1649. Look and Learn / Bernard Platman Antiquarian Collection / Bridgeman Images. Seventeenth-century woodcut.

spoken English back to their communities far more effectively than parliamentary legislation. And the Highlands benefited particularly from the new and growing market for Scottish cattle in England, while the whole kingdom sent linen south. But Anglo-Scottish relations more generally were not without their difficulties, mostly because, for all monarchs after James VI and I, being king of Scots came a long way behind being king of England. As the English began to rule the waves, founding colonies and expanding their economic reach, Scotland could only watch and envy.

CHAPTER EIGHT

UNION, ENLIGHTENMENT AND EMPIRE 1700–1800

The last decade of the seventeenth century was appalling. Years of failed harvests brought widespread famine, sending small armies of beggars from the countryside into the towns. On top of this, the entrepreneur William Paterson – who co-founded the Bank of England in 1694 – catastrophically overreached himself with the Darien Scheme. This promised investors the rich rewards of Scotland's first colony, reputedly a paradise on the Isthmus of Panama. In reality it was a disease-ridden wilderness already claimed by the Spanish. Hundreds of colonists died of sickness and starvation, and the life savings of many Scots, totalling upwards of the equivalent of £40 million today, were completely wiped out.

This was not the result of Scottish stupidity, but the fact that they had few options when it came to the scramble for colonies. King William put the interests of England and his Dutch homeland first – or more precisely, the monopolies of their respective East India Companies – and he expressly forbade English ships and colonies from trading with the upstart Scots. The Union of the Crowns had left Scotland without an effective head and unable to trade with those

William and Mary William of Orange invaded England in November 1688. He and his wife Mary, with whom he ruled jointly, were crowned five months later. Classic Image / Alamy. Allegory of the coronation of William and Mary after a work by Romeyn de Hooghe.

European powers at war with England, despite such quarrels having nothing to do with the northern kingdom.

And then there were the Stuarts. Some Scots remained loyal to the exiled branch of the royal family, including James VII and II, now in residence in Paris. Such loyalty had already brought retribution to the MacDonalds of Glencoe, who were massacred in 1692 despite having sworn allegiance to King William, albeit a few days after the deadline. Unusually, the violent deaths of nearly forty Highlanders with a reputation for unruliness caused outrage even in the Lowlands – especially as they were known to have given food and shelter to those who butchered them.

But although many Scots yearned for an economic union with England that would allow them to trade as equals, few north of the border wanted full political union. It was the English political establishment that pushed for that as both kingdoms contemplated the future after the death of the last of the children of Queen Anne, James VII and II's younger daughter. When the Scots threatened to select someone other than the English choice (George, Elector of Hanover, a descendant of James VI and I's daughter,

Beggar's badge
In times of hardship, the authorities considered beggars to be a problem and in the eighteenth century lead badges were issued to those permitted to beg. Copyright National Museums Scotland. Licensor Scran. Lead badge from Fraserburgh, late eighteenth century.

Massacre of Glencoe

Many Scots, particularly in the Highlands, remained loyal to James VII and II. In 1692 the government made an example of one clan in the infamous Massacre of Glencoe.

Peter Barritt / Alamy. Painting by James Hamilton, nineteenth century.

Elizabeth) as her heir, the English government decided to act. The extent to which they paid off members of the Scottish nobility in return for their support, especially the Duke of Hamilton who himself had a claim to the throne and supposedly led the anti-Union party, will forever remain controversial.

Under the terms of the Union Treaty, the parliaments in London and Edinburgh were dissolved and then combined as a new United Kingdom parliament sitting at Westminster. Forty-five representatives were to be elected from Scotland out of a total of 558 (489 English; 24 Welsh). Scotland's separate judicial and education system, along with the Presbyterian settlement in religion, were all preserved.

Nevertheless, the Union was unpopular in Scotland at the time, for the Scots knew they were the lesser partner in this supposed marriage of equals. And this gave Jacobitism – the campaign to restore the exiled James and his descendants – some impetus, though only in the short-term and largely among Episcopalians or Catholics or those otherwise disenchanted with the government.

As the economic benefits of Union began to take hold towards the middle of the eighteenth century, especially in the west of Scotland where Glasgow threw itself into trans-Atlantic trade, enthusiasm for the new relationship grew. The final roll of the dice for the Stuart dynasty came in 1745–6 with the arrival in Scotland of James VII and II's great-grandson, Charles Edward Stuart (Bonnie Prince Charlie). Despite wowing the Presbyterian ladies of Edinburgh, who were overjoyed at having royalty back in the capital, and sweeping all before him until Derbyshire in the heart of England, the Prince and the last Jacobite army were defeated at Culloden on 16 April 1746.

And now too the British government resolved to break the power of the Highland chiefs. Even before this last rising, troops had been sent into northern Scotland to map every glen and build roads and bridges through at least some of the most accessible. The Highlands were no longer to remain a *terra incognita*, a no-go area for royal officials. After 1745 parliament also passed laws designed to break down the barriers between Highland and Lowland society, banning Highland dress, forbidding the possession of weapons and abolishing the judicial rights that landowners across Scotland had long held, but which it was felt Highland chiefs used to control their tenants.

Banning of Highland dress
As part of government attempts to deal with the 'Highland problem', legislation was enacted banning the wearing of tartan (except in the British Army). Look and Learn / Rosenberg Collection / Bridgeman Images. Eighteenth-century engraving.

Bonnie Prince Charlie and the Cult of Heroic Failure –

Charles Edward Stuart has cast a long shadow across Scottish history, though he is most easily identifiable now as a means of selling everything from shortbread to t-shirts and kilt jackets. Despite arriving in Scotland in July 1745 without a promised French army, the prince managed to charm key Highland chiefs into rising against King George II. Largely excluded from patronage by the powerful Protestant Duke of Argyll, men like Cameron of Lochiel and Fraser of Lovat hoped they would reap the benefits of regime change, however risky the attempt.

Despite widespread opposition in the south, particularly in the towns and cities, the Jacobite army beat a government force at Prestonpans on 21 September, took Carlisle in north-west England and marched on. It was rumoured that the royal family was on the verge of leaving for Hanover when the prince reluctantly turned round, English Jacobites having failed to join him in sufficient numbers.

Pursued by the king's son, the experienced Duke of Cumberland, the two armies met on Culloden Moor outside Inverness. The Highland charge, which had proved dominant during the Covenanting Wars a century earlier, was stopped in its tracks by artillery fire. The rising was over and the Bonnie Prince, who would never set foot in Scotland again, fled for his life.

So too did his supporters, for what made this rising different were the executions and reprisals afterwards. After Culloden, government troops burned their way across the Highlands looking for escaped

Jacobites in the belief that a French army was on the way. Though some Jacobites had lost their lands before, none had lost their lives. Now over 100 were hung or beheaded, 650 died in prison and others were transported to the colonies.

Battle of Culloden Despite reaching Derby, the Jacobite army retreated over the winter of 1745-6 and was defeated at Culloden near Inverness in April 1746. Bridgeman Images. Eighteenth-century coloured line engraving by Luke Sullivan after A Heckel.

Bonnie Prince Charlie
Great-grandson of James VII
and II, Charles Edward Stuart
lived in Italy before landing
in Scotland in July 1745. He
fled after Culloden, never
recovering from the collapse
of the Stuart cause.
Bridgeman Images. Portrait by
Antonio David, 1732.

Duke of Cumberland
Prince William Augustus was the youngest son of King George II and had command of British forces at Culloden. Renowned for the brutality of the aftermath, he was nicknamed 'Butcher Cumberland'.

Copyright of the National Portrait Gallery. Portrait from the studio of Sir Joshua Reynolds, c1758.

But one of the most enduring – and ironic – legacies of Jacobitism was the large-scale absorption of the Highland soldier into the ranks of the British army.

In the long-term, however, more general social and economic trends had the most impact. Improvement – the term given to the desire to make the land and its farmers work more efficiently and profitably through a revolution in agricultural practices – slowly spread from the south-east across the country. The communal runrig system of farming was swept away and leases given to individual tenant farmers. Now they could invest in improvements that would profit them and the landowner (through increased rents), though not everyone had enough money to do it properly. And many others couldn't get a lease at all, either because there weren't enough or they couldn't afford one, forcing them and their families into nearby towns and cities or even the colonies.

Perhaps the most visible change in the 'Improved' landscape by the later eighteenth century was the neat enclosures – stone walls or banks planted with bushes of gorse or white-thorn – that split the arable land into smaller divisions. The great medieval open fields with their sinuous reverse 'S' bends, created when the oxen pulling the plough turned at the end of the rigs, vanished – though traces of them occasionally survive.

Other parts of the landscape also disappeared after the 1695 Division of Commonties Act, which authorised the break-up of lands held in common (except where they belonged to the king or royal burghs) which then were divided up among those who could claim ownership. Almost overnight, locals could no longer graze their animals where they had always taken them. Like other 'waste' grounds of heath or bog, this land might now be turned into productive fields of grain.

Perhaps the most ambitious reclamation project took place on the Carse of Stirling, a vast bog some twenty foot deep in places, at the instigation of Lord Kames of the Blair Drummond estate. In return for reduced rents, hundreds of 'Moss Lairds' flocked to dig right in to the peat, sending it floating down the River Teith and on into the River Forth between 1766 and 1865. 10,000 acres of valuable farmland were created, but the volume of waste sent downstream began to silt up the Forth so that sea-going ships could no longer sail up to Stirling. Pockets of the original Carse do remain, especially at Flanders Moss.

But arable farming was not the only type of agriculture to undergo Improvement. Bigger and meatier breeds of sheep, particularly the Cheviot, were brought in from the north of England to replace the small native ones. This appealed to some Highland proprietors, who tended to own large swathes of upland. The native cattle were pushed aside in some places in favour of large sheep-walks that, like the new farms in the south, employed only a few individuals compared to the large numbers who raised cattle on communal ground. It did not help that the new sheep managers were usually incomers from other parts of Scotland.

For those who emigrated rather than accept the changes at home, passage to the colonies was, as yet, mostly open only to those with the money for it (though, at the other extreme, there were some prepared to endure terrible conditions for a number of years as indentured labour while they paid off the money for their passage). Flora MacDonald, who helped to save Bonnie Prince Charlie from capture after Culloden, left for South Carolina with her husband in 1774, but chose the losing side again when the colonies revolted against British rule two years later in what became known as the

American Wars of Independence. Some Scots, however, made fortunes in the southern states of America or the Caribbean, growing cotton or tobacco on plantations.

Many Scots were directly involved in slave-dependent enterprises as plantation owners, surgeons or overseers, while at home some Scottish businesses produced and exported cotton cloth and salt herring to clothe and feed enslaved people. The profits of slavery often came back to Scotland, where plantation owners might buy an estate of their own or, if they already had one, like the Malcolms of Poltalloch in Argyll, invest their money in modern agricultural methods and technology. Scotland's great merchants could also now afford to build state-of-the-art mansions in cities or towns or, when Glasgow became too overcrowded, in its leafy west end. There can be no doubt that many a fortune made and wealth flowing into Scotland from the colonies and elsewhere in the British Empire was generated out of the misery of enslaved peoples for over two centuries.

Slowly but surely, housing began to improve in the countryside too, the old wattle-and-daub structures replaced with stone and mortar and, eventually, slate roofs. All these changes

Caranish, North Uist
Across Scotland the old thatch and turf buildings were slowly replaced by dressed stone and slate roofs. HES SC746888. Photograph by Erskine Beveridge, c1900.

Peat-gathering, Shetland
The long-standing tradition of peat-gathering was essential but extremely time-consuming. However, that didn't stop these women knitting at the same time.
Copyright NMS. Licensor Scran. Photograph by H B Curwen, 1902.

came slowly to the Highlands and especially the Hebrides, but the reasons for that were complex. With a rising population encouraged by some chiefs to stay on the land, the *cas chrom* or foot plough was used to grow crops on difficult terrain far more effectively than any new technology. Still other landowners discouraged their tenants from spending money on improvements by immediately raising rents, while some residents couldn't take advantage of new industries, such as the women of Inveraray in the 1790s, as they were needed for the back-breaking and time-consuming job of bringing home peats for fuel in the summer months.

But if Improvement was patchy, the pursuit of rational inquiry, in contrast to the religious fervour of the seventeenth century, began to mark Scotland out. Witch trials came to an end in 1727, by which time the country had five universities offering high quality education that included science, medicine and economics to a small number of young men – even some of modest wealth. Printing houses, journals, libraries and clubs dedicated to intellectual pursuits all played their part in cultivating an extraordinary number of thinkers and scientific innovators, from the economist Adam Smith

Glasgow University
By 1600, Scotland had four universities compared to England's two, a testament to the place of knowledge in Scottish society that later blossomed during the Enlightenment. HES DP00106452. Copy of engraving 'The Colledge of Glasgow' from *Theatrum Scotiae* by John Slezer, c1750.

Dundas House, Edinburgh
This house in the New Town belonged to Henry Dundas, who ran Scotland for the absent monarch. He encouraged the Enlightenment but opposed the abolition of slavery. Falkensteinfoto / Alamy. From original drawing by Thomas H Shepherd in *Modern Athens*, 1829.

New Town, Edinburgh
By 1800, the wealthier citizens
of Edinburgh had broken out
of the city's medieval confines
into the splendour of the
New Town.
John Bracegirdle / Alamy.

and philosopher David Hume to the engineer James Watt and geologist James Hutton. It is difficult to explain exactly why this relatively poor northern country should have played host to the Scottish Enlightenment. But there is no doubt that the rest of Europe took notice, the confidence Scotland lost in the Darien fiasco a century earlier well and truly re-found.

CHAPTER NINE
MODERN TRANSFORMATION 1800–1900

In the late eighteenth and early nineteenth century, Scotland had not just begun to 'Improve', but had become a place that well-heeled tourists from around the British Isles and even further afield were eager to experience. The Highlands held a particular fascination for both its sublime – that was the 'in' word at a time of romantic sensibilities – scenery and the supposed savage exoticism of its natives. Its most famous visitor was Queen Victoria, who adored the Highlands so much she purchased her very own retreat at Balmoral near Braemar in 1852.

At the same time, Scots were moving into towns and cities in far greater numbers even as the population in the Highlands (the north-west and the Hebrides particularly) continued to rise. In other parts of the north and west, more landlords saw the profits to be made from turning their hills over to sheep, followed by deer and game birds as the British aristocracy discovered the fun to be had from shooting them in the autumn season.

Some proprietors did not hesitate to remove their tenants wholesale, sometimes violently, from their traditional homes in relatively fertile glens to far less productive coastal areas.

Stanley Cycle Club, 1889 The invention of the safety bicycle in the 1880s replaced the precarious penny farthing and encouraged people from all walks of life to get on the move.
HES DP070849

Shooting party in Glenalmond, Perthshire, c1880

The aristocracy and entrepreneurs of Great Britain enjoyed the shooting season in Scotland, with the help of an army of attendants. HES DP035410

**Balmoral Castle,
Aberdeenshire, c1880**
Queen Victoria fell in love with
the Highlands and in 1852 her
husband acquired Balmoral as a
retreat. It is still much loved by
the royal family. HES SCI240839

These were the notorious Highland clearances, the dramatic tail-end of a process that had begun in south-east Scotland early in the eighteenth century and would ultimately transform the country from predominantly rural to urban, concentrated in the Central Belt around the Rivers Forth and Clyde. By the end of the nineteenth century, 60 per cent of the population lived in towns inhabited by more than 5,000 people.

For those who stuck it out in the Highlands, short leases combined with the tiny parcels of land many crofters – the name given to these smallholders – were forced to live and work on led to agitation that eventually became a political movement. By 1885 there were five members of parliament elected to fight for better conditions. A year later the Crofting Act defined the crofting counties, gave security of tenure to crofters within them (who did not want to own their land) and set up a Commission to ensure fair rents.

This certainly didn't solve the problem of too many people trying to eke a living out of difficult terrain and indeed encouraged some landowners to get rid of their tenants altogether, whether through emigration or

Cleared settlements on Rum, Inner Hebrides
The Highlands are littered with the remains of settlements, where inhabitants had little choice but to leave, either for southern cities or the colonies. HES DP094957

Stanley Mills, Perthshire
Even in rural areas, large industrial complexes sprang up. At Stanley, this mill harnessed the power of the River Tay to produce textiles for over 200 years. HES

removal to the industrialising south. But it at least gave a legal underpinning to the idea that the people who worked the land should have rights to it and helped to create the distinctive landscapes of these northern areas.

The opportunities to find work, albeit in often dangerous and dispiriting mines, quarries, furnaces or factories, had now increased dramatically. Given the number of Scottish scientists and inventors – not least James Watt, whose modifications to Newcomen's 1712 steam engine helped to kickstart the Industrial Revolution – it is no surprise that new technology and industrialisation were embraced with much vigour at home, just as the opportunities of Empire were taken up with great enthusiasm overseas. Any natural resource that could be transformed by fire or steam into something else was brought from far and near to mighty industrial complexes that completely dominated their surroundings. The Carron Ironworks near Falkirk was founded in 1759 and lasted until 1982. In its heyday it was one of the greatest in Europe, employing 1,000 men to keep five blast furnaces and sixteen air furnaces going day and night and encouraging landowners all over the country

James Watt
Renowned for his improvements to the steam engine, which played a key role in the Industrial Revolution, Watt himself was transformed from an instrument maker to a wealthy man. Bridgeman Images. From *Les Merveilles de la Science*, 1870.

to check their property for iron ore, ironstone or limestone.

Smaller-scale industries – mills, quarries, bleachworks for cotton – popped up everywhere, transforming hillsides and river banks that might be quieter now than they were then. Stanley Mills near Perth and New Lanark are surviving examples of these major enterprises. But it was coal – dug ever deeper to serve a rising Lowland population – that would define the landscapes of the Central Belt. And in Glasgow there was the rise of shipbuilding on the River Clyde.

Glasgow's prosperity – and its growth – had begun with the tobacco brought in from plantations in North America and the Caribbean, but it was the dredging of the Clyde in 1768 that brought even greater prospects. Large ocean-going ships were able to come right up into the city, where the banks of the Clyde became renowned for shipbuilding. But where Glasgow had been lauded as beautiful in the early eighteenth century, a hundred years later the homes of the urban poor east of the city centre were a wretched sight.

Edinburgh, on the other hand, became much improved around the turn of the nineteenth century as it finally broke out into a beautifully designed New Town to the north of the original medieval city. But as the countesses and professionals fled the squalor of the high-rises, they left the poor behind and it was easy for those with wealth and power to forget what poverty looked like.

Nevertheless, poverty and education happily co-existed in modern Scotland. By 1808, 189 schools had been established in the Highlands by the Society in Scotland for Propagating Christian Knowledge (SSPCK), founded in 1709 and dedicated to stamping out 'uncivilised' behaviour, not to mention Jacobitism, through Presbyterian education. Though native speakers were used by the SSPCK, many Highland communities were extremely suspicious of a movement animated by Lowland prejudice towards the Gaelic language and Gaelic culture.

In the Lowlands, subscription libraries were set up from the mid-eighteenth century and patronised even by men labouring long hours in mines and fields (and possibly some women too). Public libraries, on the other hand, were less easily established because of the need for taxes for their construction and upkeep. Most of the early ones were built with money gifted by Andrew Carnegie, one of the world's richest

Scott Monument, Edinburgh, c1890
This gothic spire dominates Princes Street, reminding natives and visitors of the contribution of Sir Walter Scott to literature.
HES SC466193

men, who had gone to America and made a fortune in steel. The first Carnegie library was established in his hometown of Dunfermline in Fife in 1883.

The thirst for books and journals on all manner of subjects was amply filled by Scottish publishers and booksellers. Agricultural societies across the country often produced their own publications, which helped to spread the newest ideas quickly and effectively. But the growing middle classes were thirsty for entertainment as well as edification, a market that the novels of the Borders lawyer Sir Walter Scott helped to satisfy, doing much to establish historical fiction as a literary genre at the same time.

An increasingly literate population was one that knew and understood what was happening in the world, through newspapers, books and chapbooks (small paper-covered booklets). The French revolution of 1789 was a major challenge to the establishment across Europe and surely provoked a reaction among Scots whose recent forebears had fought for the freedom to practise their religion according to their own consciences, whether or not their king agreed.

After 1789, it was not just religion that came under public scrutiny, but the whole hierarchical

Sir Walter Scott and the writing of Scottish history – Walter Scott (1771–1832) not only helped to create the genre of historical fiction, but also kickstarted a romantic interpretation of Scotland's past that is still influential today. He spent much of his childhood in the Scottish Borders, where he heard and loved local stories and folklore. Trained as a lawyer, he continued to devour all kinds of literature, including James Macpherson's infamous 'translation' of an ancient Gaelic epic poem – supposedly by the bard Ossian, but widely believed to be a forgery. At the age of fifteen, he was overawed at meeting Robert Burns, and ten years later, he began to publish his own material, including the Border stories of his youth. His first novel, *Waverley*, was published anonymously in 1814. Given his class and upbringing, it is not surprising that Scott was a defender of the status quo and he is credited as founder of the Romantic Movement characterised by nostalgia for a simpler, better past. However, Scott's fiction was often a reaction to, and exploration of, the impact of the economic and social upheavals – not least the struggle that finally brought about the Great Reform Act of 1832. As a passionate advocate for Scottish history, in 1818 Sir Walter succeeded in bringing the Honours of Scotland (Scotland's Crown Jewels) back into the open, after they had been locked in a trunk in Edinburgh Castle for over a hundred years. Four years later, he presided over the entry of a tartan-clad George IV into Edinburgh, a spectacle that was designed to draw a line under the bloody conflicts of earlier centuries.

The meeting of Burns and Scott in Sciennes House, Edinburgh Scott was a teenager when he met Burns, who, despite being the toast of Edinburgh society, rarely made enough money from his writings. Lebrecht Authors / Bridgeman Images. From the 1893 painting by Charles Martin Hardie.

nature of society. As the great Scottish poet Robert Burns fervently hoped: 'For a' that, an' a' that, It's coming yet for a' that. That Man to Man, the world o'er, Shall brothers be for a' that.' But there was little in the way of violent protest, however desperate conditions became, and supporters of revolutionary ideas were ruthlessly dealt with by the authorities.

And yet again one of the most important challenges to the status quo came in the religious, rather than political, sphere. It had long been a bone of contention that the appointment of church ministers was in the hands of local landowners, but moderates in the General Assembly were unwilling to challenge this arrangement. In 1833, however, the Assembly consisted of a majority of Evangelical ministers who passed an Act allowing local congregations to veto appointments. The courts upheld the rights of landowners to 'intrude' their choice, and the stage was set for a showdown.

It came ten years later when large numbers of ministers and their congregations left the Church of Scotland to set up the Free Church, driven by a combination of middle-class social protest against the power of the aristocracy and nationalist sentiment that blamed decisions taken in London for the crisis. The Disruption, as this mass walk-out was called, divided communities but, somewhat ironically, encouraged considerable investment in the established Church. It also promoted a more diverse range of views on religious questions, including a greater tolerance of Catholicism. Most issues were resolved and the Church reunited in 1929, but the Free Church continued to hold sway in the Highlands, where it had a reputation for ultra-conservatism.

But society was changing and questions were now asked about aspects of public life – patronage, nepotism and the purchasing of state offices – that had been perfectly acceptable before the nineteenth century. Since the abolition of the Privy Council in 1708, Scotland had been largely left to its own devices, controlled by a series of political managers, most famously Henry Dundas, Viscount Melville (1742–1811), whose nickname was King Harry the Ninth. Local concerns were dealt with locally, albeit by the usual entrenched interests, and the British state was generally kept at arm's length.

But the great changes that came to nineteenth-century England were also visited on Scotland, sometimes to greater effect. The first

Reform Act of 1832 – the result of decades of campaigning against the unfairness of the electoral system that included the massacre of hundreds of people at Peterloo in Manchester in 1819 – expanded the Scottish electorate by 1,400 per cent (compared with an 80 per cent increase in England), allowing the middle classes to take their place in politics alongside the traditional elites.

Though progress to extend the franchise further down the social scale was slow, the peaceful movements of the 1860s designed to put pressure on the government helped to foster a strong British patriotism – loyalty to Queen Victoria was most explicit – alongside a vigorous Scottish patriotism that saw William Wallace co-opted as a working class, pro-Union hero. These protests were large events, especially in Glasgow, which boasted participants and spectators numbering up to 100,000.

But the aim of the movement was to allow more men to vote. Few were campaigning to extend the same rights to women, even as late as the third Reform Act (1884–5). The explosion in jobs that attended the Industrial Revolution brought opportunities that had often been

Scottish suffragettes, 1908
As elsewhere in the UK, Scottish women campaigned hard for the right to vote. Here suffragettes welcome Mary Phillips (standing third from left) on her release from prison.
Heritage Image Partnership Ltd / Alamy.

denied to women in recent centuries. The financial independence that followed allowed wives to leave abusive husbands far more readily than in the past, while easier access to coal, for example, slowly but surely took them away from the time-consuming tyranny of having to bring peats home. Though the great drive to spread schools around the country after the Reformation had been aimed at boys, the 1872 Education (Scotland) Act made primary education compulsory for all children, regardless of income, under the auspices of 1,000 school boards.

Middle-class women had played their part in the great debates of the day. But, despite their prominence in the campaign to abolish slavery particularly, they failed to make any headway in getting the vote in 1832. By the 1860s the women's suffrage movement began to flourish with Scottish suffragettes suffering from the same hostility, including forced feeding in prison, as their English counterparts. Like them, too, they finally received equal treatment with men in 1928.

But despite the many positive developments of this century, disease and death were still commonplace. The Potato Famine of 1846 and

1847 may have brought about far fewer deaths in the Highlands – where potatoes formed up to two-thirds of the diet – than in Ireland, thanks to various support initiatives. But it proved yet another reason for many thousands to leave the area altogether.

It was urban diseases, and cholera in particular, that prompted real change. Though the poor – living cheek by jowl in intensely unsanitary conditions – were most at risk, the discovery in the mid-nineteenth century that cholera was spread via contaminated water, infecting across social boundaries, led to considerable investment in bringing clean water to the cities. Glasgow moved first, after an outbreak in 1848–9 killed 4,000 people. Loch Katrine – renowned as the setting for Sir Walter's Scott's romantic poem *The Lady of the Lake* – was dammed, its water carried 34 miles through aqueducts, tunnels and bridges to Glasgow from 1859. The next outbreak of cholera six years later killed only 53 people in the city, prompting Edinburgh and Dundee to follow suit. At last technology could be seen to work for the greater good, not just the profits of a few.

CHAPTER TEN
A VERY MODERN SCOTLAND 1900–2000s

The dramatic convulsions of the twentieth century affected Scotland as elsewhere in the United Kingdom, though political developments had a particularly Scottish slant to them. From the middle of the century, the nation seemed to falter, unsure of its future in the face of the loss of the great manufacturing industries of the Central Belt and of the British Empire, where so many Scots had worked as soldiers and administrators. But by the end of the century, Scotland had a parliament of its own in Edinburgh and a renewed sense of optimism. Whether this is sufficient answer to global economic forces, along with the trans-national threats of climate change, will be the crucial question of this current century.

The pace of change in the twentieth century was quite extraordinary. The Scottish population was booming, increasing from around 1 million in 1700 to 4.5 million by 1900, around the same as it is now. At the start of the century, the owners of Scottish capital and the country's productive resources controlled shipping lines, railway companies, mining enterprises and huge areas of agricultural land across the globe. They were highly influential in London, where economic

The Scottish Parliament, Edinburgh Designed by Enric Miralles and set within Edinburgh's UNESCO World Heritage Site, the parliament building was opened by the Queen in 2004. DTR Photography / Alamy.

policy was devised. At the same time, Glasgow – one of the great cities of shipbuilding and of Empire – contained some of the worst slums in Europe. Despite the building of the Loch Katrine reservoir to pump fresh water into the city, which dramatically reduced the rates of cholera, infectious diseases like tuberculosis remained endemic and infant mortality tragically high.

But, despite the appalling poverty affecting more Scots than the UK average, there was relatively little social unrest in the years leading up to the First World War. Though the Scottish Labour Party was founded in 1888 and the Scottish Trades Union Congress nine years later, there was little support for socialism, and social stability was fostered by a widespread faith in a British state tempered by distinctive Scottish traditions. Even if some wealthy men and women worked to expose and improve the terrible conditions of the urban slums, those who did not dwell there (even if they made their money from the labour of those who did) often preferred their culture to focus on more romantic rural imagery emphasising the 'natural' order of things and with a premium placed on an idealised past.

Writers like John Buchan and J M Barrie were happy to satisfy that need, while a distinctive

John Brown's Shipyard in Clydebank, Glasgow, 1935
Glasgow's shipyards were among the busiest in the world, building great liners like the *Queen Mary.*
HES SCI257773

type of Scottish architecture – mock baronial – gave those who could afford it a slice of what the rich had lived in for centuries (albeit with mod cons like electricity and running water) or permitted town authorities to insert a dose of grandeur into their civic buildings. On the other hand, painters and designers like Charles Rennie Mackintosh and J D Fergusson were determined to let in colour and light, a passionate disavowal of the overbearing symbols of hierarchy and obedience preferred by the elites.

Change came with the First World War, not least as bargaining power moved from the owners of capital to the workforce. Because the Labour movement had such shallow roots in Scotland, workers on Clydeside (the heart of Glasgow's great shipbuilding industry) began to organise themselves more radically than the official unions, with men and women co-ordinating mass rent strikes and other forms of collective action. Across the Central Belt, those used to the deference of their workers found them aggressive and uncooperative. With the Russian Revolution of 1917 uppermost in the authorities' minds, tanks were sent in to restore order in Glasgow in January 1919, but left-wing politics now came naturally to the urban working classes, who had previously voted Liberal.

There was certainly work to be done by all political parties. The post-war economy did little to help those who had paid such a heavy price in the war years. Stagnation and contraction throughout the 1920s resulted in over half a million Scots, most of them young, leaving for England or further afield, the largest migration in the nation's history. The loss of both workers and consumers only made the crisis deeper. Back home, infant mortality in the 1930s was still among the worst in Europe.

Most of the female working population between the wars was unmarried – it was still expected that women would give up their jobs in exchange for a wedding ring. It was then only a matter of time until their days were fully occupied in bringing up families, often of five or more, as both Protestant and Catholic churches remained resolutely opposed to any form of birth control. For the unmarried, given the numbers of war dead as well as emigration, female employment actually rose in the 1930s, predominantly in shops and domestic service, with only around 4 per cent qualifying as teachers, which was effectively the only profession open to women.

**Singer Factory,
Clydebank, c1934**
Great industrial complexes
were also built on the Clyde,
including the Singer Factory,
capable of producing 13,000
sewing machines a week.
HES DP048412

And not all industries were entirely male. The sewing machine factory at Clydebank to the west of Glasgow, with its famous illuminated clock tower, was the first plant set up in Europe by the American Singer company, thanks to a plentiful supply of skilled labour and iron foundries. Opened in 1885 (having occupied a smaller site at Bridgeton since 1873), the factory employed 11,500 workers at its peak, producing 80 per cent of the world's sewing machines. Fathers, sons and daughters often worked there. It was not immune to demands for better conditions, with almost the entire workforce coming out in support of twelve women cabinet polishers expected to work longer for less in a famous strike of 1911. But, as with other manufacturers in Scotland, Singer could no longer compete with cheaper products made elsewhere in the second half of the twentieth century. Both the Clydebank factory and another in Dundee closed in the early 1980s.

The rise of left-wing politics coincided with the emergence of another political force, Scottish nationalism. Questions about the Union began among a new generation of Scottish writers led by Hugh MacDiarmid, who felt the crushing weight of failure in the aftermath of the General Strike of 1926, when thousands of industrial workers downed tools and threatened a revolution along the lines of the one in Russia in 1917. The growing use of the Scots language reflected both a rejection of English as a form of colonialism and a desire for a distinctive Scottish voice. These writers certainly did not all agree, either in their subject matter or in the solutions they offered. But they did focus on contemporary issues, rather than looking to the past as their immediate predecessors tended to do. In 1928, members of the Independent Labour Party set up the National Party of Scotland, followed three years later by the founding of a more establishment version, the Scottish Party. These two groups came together in 1934 as the Scottish National Party.

Despite the upheavals of the previous 150 years, the countryside was not immune to further change. In the crofting counties, central planning was adopted on land bought by the state, which created new smallholdings, particularly in the Hebrides. Similar government schemes took place in the Lowlands, especially as part of the promise of 'Homes fit for Heroes' after the First World War, which provided houses built on between two and four acres, based on a standard official design. Most were sold off to their existing tenants in the 1930s, but some are still visible on the edges of towns and cities.

Improvement was now everywhere – fields mostly lay in neat, straight lines, and stone farmhouses and farm buildings were usually built round a central courtyard. Wire fencing – much cheaper and easier to put up – came on the market in the mid-nineteenth century, changing the look of the landscape once more, though stone was still used for dykes, particularly in the north-east where it was plentiful.

And although Improvement had initially forced those farmers who couldn't get leases to move away, in the nineteenth century there was still a great need for farm workers to feed a rising population. The farmer and his family usually lived in the big house set adjacent to the farmyard, built some distance away from the row of stone cottages that were home to his labourers. Around the turn of the twentieth century, he and his wife might still sit around one long table with their 'family' of workers in the farmhouse at mealtimes. But by the 1930s, the numbers of labourers declined dramatically as mechanisation began to create a very different farming landscape and way of life.

After the Second World War, horses were replaced by machines as part of a government drive to provide cheap food at a time of continued food rationing. Now hedges were removed to create larger fields to accommodate ever bigger tractors, threshers and combine harvesters. But such mechanical beasts required fewer hands, and farmhouse kitchens began to empty. By the end of the century, farmer and shepherd required only their dogs and a quad bike to manage huge tracts of land. This might have improved profits in a highly competitive industry, but there is no denying the loneliness of the farming life now, which once resounded with the riotousness of old and young coming together to make light of back-breaking work.

Another industry to alter the face of the Scottish landscape was forestry. Since the later Middle Ages, the Scottish government had worried about the lack of trees in the Lowlands, though the Highlands long boasted large tracts of forest, which attracted those needing charcoal, particularly for iron smelting, from the eighteenth century. But the First World War consumed huge amounts of timber, much of it from relatively new plantations on

Tala Reservoir, Peeblesshire

In the drive for clean water, numerous Scottish rivers were dammed. This reservoir was built in 1899 and was soon surrounded by fast-growing conifers for forestry.
HES DP033547

**Hand-milking,
Fair Isle, c1950**

Scottish farming industrialised
and mechanised in the drive
for cheap food prompted
by the Second World War.
Much of the population no
longer worked on the land.
Copyright National Museums
Scotland. Licensor Scran.

Hughes Microelectronics Factory, Glenrothes, 1975
One of the many revolutions of the twentieth century was the arrival of women en masse in the workplace.
Copyright The Scotsman Publications Ltd. Licensor Scran.

private estates. In response, the UK government founded the Forestry Commission in 1919 to create state-owned forests to try to restore self-sufficiency. While there was some resistance to large-scale planting in England, especially in the Lake District, it was comparatively easy and certainly cheaper to purchase bare hillsides in Scotland, which were then of little interest to farmers. By 1939, the Commission was the biggest landowner in Britain, having acquired 9 per cent of the total Scottish landmass, which was just as well, given that the Second World War was about to make further inroads into the nation's forests.

By the end of the war, however, the dawn of the Nuclear Age meant there was no longer a need to maintain a strategic reserve of timber to construct, among many other things, hangars, barracks, bridges and shipping crates necessary for traditional warfare. Post-war governments wanted the Forestry Commission to make money out of their trees, but the drive for cheap food production on the lower, better land meant that new ground purchased for forestry tended to be on ever higher and more difficult soils. Machinery did help to push costs down but as more and more people ventured into the Scottish countryside and the Forestry Commission itself encouraged them to camp and walk on some of their land, dissatisfaction grew with regimented plantations filled with row upon row of the same kind of tree – usually the North American Sitka Spruce. The growth of environmental awareness began to affect Commission policy as native tree species were encouraged in some parts of the forest estate.

But despite the jobs brought by forestry, the twentieth-century story for much of the Highlands was the very opposite of the Lowlands, with people still flooding away from the glens and islands as industries and jobs continued to decline. Even the immense seasonal migration of herring – the silver darlings – which had boomed in the nineteenth century and into the twentieth, providing work for over 10,000 boats and many a young fisher lass and lad from all around Scotland's northern coasts, was over by the end of the Second World War.

It was a problem that successive governments tried to solve, but distances from markets meant that most traditional industries could not compete cost-effectively (though this was becoming a general trend across Scotland after the Second World War). Attempts to halt

**Herring gutters,
Peterhead, c1900**
Herring fishing was once a
major industry that employed
both men and women in
large numbers. Copyright
Arbuthnot Museum.
Peterhead. Licensor Scran.

emigration prompted a number of enterprises aimed at creating work, most particularly a hydro scheme, power station and aluminium works at Kinlochleven and another aluminium smelter and pulp and paper works at Corpach, all near Fort William.

Most of these were gone by the end of the twentieth century, but the hydro scheme at Kinlochleven still makes electricity from the water carried from Blackwater Reservoir four miles away. Indeed most Scottish rivers and lochs are affected one way or another by large-scale hydro schemes begun around the end of the Second World War, many of which engulfed farms and villages to create huge reservoirs.

As the UK, and Scotland with it, became less competitive in global markets, many of the great industries that had helped power it into the first rank of industrialising nations began to falter. The Carron Ironworks closed in 1982 after 223 years. Ten years later the Ravenscraig hot strip mill south-east of Glasgow – like the Carron works the largest in Europe in its time – also closed its doors, with the loss of over 10,000 jobs directly and indirectly.

By then most of the great shipbuilding companies had already shut or been severely

The new Scottish parliament – The Labour government that came to power in 1997 immediately delivered on a promise to allow a vote on restoring a parliament to Edinburgh and on 12 May 1999 that parliament met for the first time in nearly 300 years. The design for a building to house MSPs (members of the Scottish parliament), civil servants and support staff was put out to tender, a competition won by the Spanish architect Enric Miralles. It soon attracted controversy, however, not least as costs began to spiral.

Despite some criticism, since its opening in October 2004, the Scottish parliament building has won a number of awards and has become an iconic part of the Edinburgh landscape with stunning views onto the neighbouring Holyrood Park. Much thought was also given to the interior layout, particularly the main debating chamber. Unlike the UK parliament at Westminster, where the government and opposition parties sit directly across from one another in an adversarial pose, seating in the Scottish chamber forms a semi-circle to encourage MSPs to work together.

In addition to passing legislation and the day-to-day business of government, the Scottish parliament building plays host to events and exhibitions, encouraging the public to come inside. In the years since it was opened by Elizabeth II, the Scottish parliament has become a focal point for national life as well as a distinctive presence opposite the queen's official Scottish residence at Holyrood Palace, and it is hard now to imagine Edinburgh without it.

Debating chamber, Scottish parliament To encourage consensual politics, MSPs do not sit opposite each other as at Westminster. Copyright Scottish Parliament. Licensor Scran.

the scottish parliament

cut back. John Brown's shipyard in Clydebank, which had once built great liners like the *QE2* as well as ships for the British Navy, staggered on until 2001 making rigs and exploration modules for the oil industry in the North Sea. But such ventures no longer provided secure, decent jobs for life for thousands of young men. The image and identity of the Scots in general, and Glaswegians in particular, as a proud manufacturing people lay in tatters.

But even if this marked the death knell of Scotland's great manufacturing history, the later twentieth century was also a time of regeneration and optimism after the privations of war, as well as heralding ever greater challenges to the status quo. Urban overpopulation and the terrible state of houses across Scotland's towns and cities led to major government initiatives to deal with the many ills that lurked in and around overcrowded, rubbish-strewn tenements. The most dramatic was the creation of five New Towns, two near Glasgow (Cumbernauld and East Kilbride), another at Irvine further west, one near Edinburgh (Livingston) and a fifth set in the coal-mining heart of Fife (Glenrothes).

These were fully designed landscapes providing everything, from green spaces to

Cumbernauld, North Lanarkshire, 1962
Though they have not always aged well, the New Towns of the 1960s took a bold approach to urban planning.
Copyright The Scotsman Publications Ltd. Licensor Scran.

schools and shops, that its inhabitants might need. But they were based on the contemporary rationale that men were usually the main or sole breadwinners and worked close to where they lived. Within only a few decades, this would no longer be the case. However, the emphasis on the health of all Scotland's citizens did result in many changes for the better, even if what was once new and suitable becomes, over time, dilapidated and no longer fit for purpose, requiring fresh investment and new ideas that have not always been forthcoming.

New ideas were also needed in other, less tangible but vitally important, areas of Scottish life. By the later twentieth century, the Gaelic language – and with it millennia of history and culture – had almost disappeared. Children were taught exclusively in English and parents began to view their native tongue as detrimental to 'getting on'. With Scottish government policy since 1999 promoting practical measures and a much greater appreciation of the language's value to the nation as a whole, there are some grounds for optimism. Though only 1.1 per cent of Scots claimed to speak Gaelic in 2011 (1,000 fewer than 2001), it had not declined among the young.

And at last, too, some parts of the Highlands are increasing in population, though mostly thanks to those wishing to retire to peace and quiet. The trick will be to attract more young people to stay rather than move away. The region is also a victim of its own success, facing intense pressure in certain areas because of its popularity as a globally renowned tourist destination. The North Coast 500 – essentially the rebranding of a route through stunning scenery beyond Inverness – has brought a new lease of life to many businesses. But locals are also finding it has an impact on their daily lives just as in Venice or Barcelona.

Ironically, too, given its longer history, the Highlands have become the 'face' of Scotland now that the nation's image as a major contributor to the economic power of Great Britain in the heyday of industrialisation and empire is no longer tenable. Tartan – once banned if used in Highland dress for giving succour to Jacobite tendencies – is now the manufactured symbol of Scottishness encompassing everything from a genuine Highland family to a football team or global business.

Scotland is also renowned throughout the world for whisky (Scotch, if you must), which was forced underground in previous centuries to avoid prohibitive excise duties and is now worth an estimated £4.7 billion per year, totalling 21 per cent of all UK food and drink exports. And this is before mentioning the biggest economic development of the later twentieth century – oil – which has made a mammoth contribution to UK finances since the 1960s, as well as transforming the small town of Aberdeen into an international oil hub. Though production peaked in 1999, the North Sea still satisfies most of the UK's oil and gas needs.

The Scottish landscape is also changing, not so much in the Central Belt which has undergone the most transformation over the last two centuries, but in the hills. There new forests are being planted, not of trees, but of wind turbines as Scotland attempts to move away from carbon-based energy sources by 2050, even as new oil fields are being developed offshore. There are still terrible disparities, too, between that laudable environmental ambition and the appalling poverty affecting more than half a million Scots.

In the last fifty years, the political landscape has also been transformed. Since the 1950s,

Oil rig Cromarty Firth
In 2017-18, oil and gas fields in Scotland accounted for 96 per cent of UK crude oil. Companies are obliged by law to remove old rigs from the sea.
Jordi Ventura / Alamy.

Windfarm and Carbisdale Castle, Sutherland
In 2018 over 75 per cent of Scotland's electricity consumption was met by renewable sources, including hydro and wind turbines.
Geopix / Alamy.

support for the Conservative Party has declined from 50 per cent to less than 20 per cent, initially to the benefit of the Labour Party, which wielded considerable power at both local and national level. That power looked unbreakable in 1997, with the election of a Labour government in the aftermath of the Thatcher era, a period of twenty years of Conservative rule that many Scots felt they had not voted for.

Though Scotland remains part of the family of nations forming the UK, Holyrood controls areas such as health, housing, education and rural affairs. Since 2010, however, the Labour Party's hegemony in both UK and Scottish elections appears in decline, mostly in favour of the Scottish National Party. Scotland's political future is far from certain, but depends in large part – as it did in 1707 – on events in England.

Huge challenges undoubtedly face this proud, ancient nation on the very edge of Europe, as they have done in the past. But there should be no doubting its courage and ingenuity in meeting them as new chapters are added to Scotland's complex and fascinating story.

Kings of Alba

843–58	Kenneth I
858–62	Donald I
862–77	Constantine I
877–8	Aed
878–89	Eochaid with Giric
889–900	Donald II
900–43	Constantine II
943–54	Malcolm I
954–62	Indulf
962–6	Dubh
966–71	Culen
971–95	Kenneth II
995–7	Constantine III
997–1005	Kenneth III
1005–34	Malcolm II
1034–40	Duncan I
1040–57	Macbeth
1058	Lulach

Canmore Dynasty

1058–93	Malcolm III
1093–4	Donald III
1094	Duncan II
1094–7	Donald III
1097–1107	Edgar
1107–24	Alexander I
1124–53	David I
1153–65	Malcolm IV
1165–1214	William I
1214–49	Alexander II
1249–86	Alexander III
1286–92	*Interregnum (rule by guardians of Scotland)*
1292–6	John (Balliol)
1296–1306	*Interregnum (Scotland left without a resident king after Balliol forced to abdicate)*
1306–29	Robert I (the Bruce)
1329–71	David II

Stewart/Stuart

1371–90	Robert II
1390–1406	Robert III
1406–37	James I
1437–60	James II
1460–88	James III
1488–1513	James IV
1513–42	James V
1542–67	Mary, Queen of Scots
1567–1625	James VI, also James I of England from 1603
1625–49	Charles I
1649–85	Charles II
1685–89	James VII
1689–94	Mary II
1689–1702	William II
1702–14	Anne

Hanover

1714–27	George I
1727–60	George II
1760–1820	George III
1820–30	George IV
1830–7	William IV
1837–1901	Victoria

Saxe-Coburg & Gotha/Windsor

1901–10	Edward VII
1910–36	George V
1936	Edward VIII
1936–52	George VI
1952–	Elizabeth II

kings and queens

Non-Fiction

The Wars of Scotland, 1214–1371
Michael Brown (Edinburgh University Press, 2004)

Impaled Upon a Thistle: Scotland since 1880
Ewen A Cameron (Edinburgh University Press, 2010)

Scotland Reformed, 1488–1587
Jane E A Dawson (Edinburgh University Press, 2007)

The Scottish Clearances: A History of the Dispossessed, 1600–1900
T M Devine (Allen Lane, 2018)

The Scottish Nation: A Modern History
T M Devine (Penguin, 2012)

From Caledonia to Pictland: Scotland to 795
James Fraser (Edinburgh University Press, 2009)

The New Penguin History of Scotland: From the Earliest Times to the Present Day
eds R A Houston and W W J Knox (Penguin, 2002)

Set Adrift Upon the World: The Sutherland Clearances
Jim Hunter (Birlinn, 2015)

Industry, Reform and Empire: Scotland, 1790–1880
Iain Hutchison (Edinburgh University Press, 2020)

Domination and Lordship: Scotland, 1070–1230
Richard Oram (Edinburgh University Press, 2011)

A History of Scotland's Landscapes
Fiona Watson with Piers Dixon (Historic Environment Scotland, 2018)

From Pictland to Alba: Scotland, 789–1070
Alex Woolf (Edinburgh University Press, 2007)

Fiction

Sunset Song
Lewis Grassic Gibbon (Polygon, 2006)

And the Land Lay Still
James Robertson (Penguin, 2011)

Acknowledgements

I would like to thank Christine Wilson, Oliver Brookes and Alasdair Burns from the HES Publications team. Thanks also go to HES staff including Nicki Scott and her colleagues in Cultural Resources – Stefan Sagrott, Morvern French, Judith Anderson – and Derek Smart and the photographic and digitising services. The text was proofread by Mairi Sutherland and indexed by Linda Sutherland.

Shetland

Orkney

scotland

Hebrides

Inverness

The Highlands

Aberdeen

Stirling

Glasgow
Edinburgh

The Lowlands

Northern Ireland

England

Index

Index